Frommer's®

Madrid
day BY day™

2nd Edition

by Mary-Ann Gallagher

John Wiley & Sons, Inc.

Contents

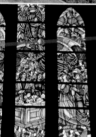

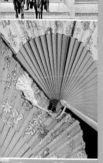

Editorial Director: Kelly Regan

Production Manager: Daniel Mersey

Commissioning Editor: Fiona Quinn

Development Editor: Donald Strachan

Content Editor: Erica Peters

Photo Research: Richard H Fox, Cherie Cincilla, Jill Emeny

Cartography: Simonetta Giori

British Library Cataloguing in Publication Data

A catalogue record for this book is available from the British Library

ISBN 978-1-119-99414-5 (pbk), ISBN 978-1-119-99477-0 (ebk),
ISBN 978-1-119-99476-3 (ebk), ISBN 978-1-119-97258-7 (ebk)

Typeset by Wiley Indianapolis Composition Services

Printed and bound in China by RR Donnelley

5   4   3   2   1

A Note from the Editorial Director

Organizing your time. That's what this guide is all about.

Other guides give you long lists of things to see and do and then expect you to fit the pieces together. The Day by Day guides are different. These guides tell you the best of everything, and then they show you how to see it *in the smartest, most time-efficient way*. Our authors have designed detailed itineraries organized by time, neighborhood, or special interest. And each tour comes with a bulleted map that takes you from stop to stop.

Hoping to visit world-class art museums, be dazzled by the vast Royal Palace, or try superb tapas at traditional taverns? Planning a walk along the Gran Vía, or plotting a day of funfilled activities with the kids? Whatever your interest or schedule, the Day by Days give you the smartest routes to follow. Not only do we take you to the top attractions, hotels, and restaurants, but we also help you access those special moments that locals get to experience—those "finds" that turn tourists into travelers.

The Day by Days are also your top choice if you're looking for one complete guide for all your travel needs. The best hotels and restaurants for every budget, the greatest shopping values, the wildest nightlife—it's all here.

Why should you trust our judgment? Because our authors personally visit each place they write about. They're an independent lot who say what they think and would never include places they wouldn't recommend to their best friends. They're also open to suggestions from readers. If you'd like to contact them, please send your comments our way at feedback@frommers.com, and we'll pass them on.

Enjoy your Day by Day guide—the most helpful travel companion you can buy. And have the trip of a lifetime.

Warm regards,

Kelly Regan

Kelly Regan, Editorial Director
Frommer's Travel Guides

About the Author

Mary-Ann Gallagher is a British travel writer who has spent many years in Spain, and has written dozens of guidebooks for publishers around the world. She now lives in Barcelona with her family, but visits the captivating Spanish capital as often as possible.

Acknowledgments

Muchas gracias to Susannah, Eduardo and Max for making Madrid even more fun than usual, and to Sally and Tara for top tips. Thanks to all at Frommer's, especially Fiona Quinn for all her hard work, patience and kindness.

Advisory & Disclaimer

Travel information can change quickly and unexpectedly, and we strongly advise you to confirm important details locally before traveling, including information on visas, health and safety, traffic and transport, accommodations, shopping, and eating out. We also encourage you to stay alert while traveling and to remain aware of your surroundings. Avoid civil disturbances, and keep a close eye on cameras, purses, wallets, and other valuables.

While we have endeavored to ensure that the information contained within this guide is accurate and up-to-date at the time of publication, we make no representations or warranties with respect to the accuracy or completeness of the contents of this work and specifically disclaim all warranties, including without limitation warranties of fitness for a particular purpose. We accept no responsibility or liability for any inaccuracy or errors or omissions, or for any inconvenience, loss, damage, costs, or expenses of any nature whatsoever incurred or suffered by anyone as a result of any advice or information contained in this guide.

The inclusion of a company, organization, or website in this guide as a service provider and/or potential source of further information does not mean that we endorse them or the information they provide. Be aware that information provided through some websites may be unreliable and can change without notice. Neither the publisher nor author shall be liable for any damages arising herefrom.

Star Ratings, Icons & Abbreviations

Every hotel, restaurant, and attraction listing in this guide has been ranked for quality, value, service, amenities, and special features using a **star-rating** system. Hotels, restaurants, attractions, shopping, and nightlife are rated on a scale of zero stars (recommended) to three stars (exceptional). In addition to the star-rating system, we also use a **kids** icon to point out the best bets for families. Within each tour, we recommend cafes, bars, or restaurants where you can take a break. Each of these stops appears in a shaded box marked with a coffee-cup-shaped bullet ☕.

The following **abbreviations** are used for credit cards:

AE	American Express	DISC	Discover	V Visa
DC	Diners Club	MC	MasterCard	

Travel Resources at Frommers.com

Frommer's travel resources don't end with this guide. Frommer's website, **www.frommers.com**, has travel information on more than 4,000 destinations. We update features regularly, giving you access to the most current trip-planning information and the best airfare, lodging, and car-rental bargains. You can also listen to podcasts, connect with other Frommers.com members through our active-reader forums, share your travel photos, read blogs from guidebook editors and fellow travelers, and much more.

How to Contact Us

In researching this book, we discovered many wonderful places—hotels, restaurants, shops, and more. We're sure you'll find others. Please tell us about them, so we can share the information with your fellow travelers in upcoming editions. If you were disappointed with a recommendation, we'd love to know that, too. Please e-mail: frommers@wiley.com or write to:

Frommer's Madrid Day by Day, 2nd Edition
John Wiley & Sons, Inc. • 111 River St. • Hoboken, NJ 07030-5774

12 Favorite
Moments

12 **Favorite Moments**

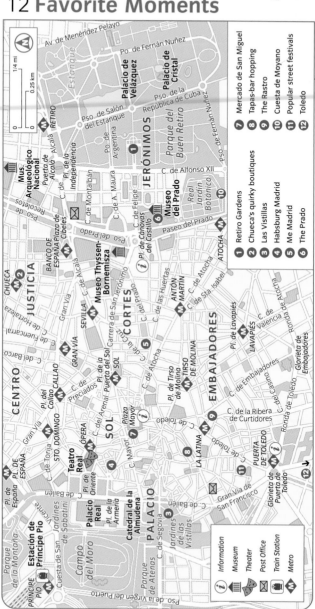

1 Retiro Gardens
2 Chueca's quirky boutiques
3 Las Vistillas
4 Habsburg Madrid
5 Me Madrid
6 The Prado
7 Mercado de San Miguel
8 Tapas-bar hopping
9 The Rastro
10 Cuesta de Moyano
11 Popular street festivals
12 Toledo

Information
Museum
Theater
Post Office
Train Station
Metro

Previous page: Plaza Mayor.

ew European capitals can compare with Madrid when it comes to showing visitors a good time. The city boasts three of the world's best art museums, a gigantic royal palace, a beautifully preserved old quarter, and hundreds of fabulous tapas bars and restaurants. Expect the fun to go on all night: Madrileños are called *"los gatos"* (the cats) for a reason.

❶ Lazing in the Retiro Gardens. Madrid's beautiful public park is a green expanse full of shady pathways, fountains, and dainty pavilions. I come with my son to feed the carp at the boating lake, and then enjoy a picnic under the trees. *See p 95.*

❷ Shopping in Chueca's quirky boutiques. The smart shops of Salamanca are more famous, but I prefer to amble around the chic little boutiques of boho Chueca. *See p 61.*

❸ Watching the sun set over the Sierras. I love to sit at a terrace cafe in Las Vistillas and watch the sun sink behind the distant mountains and set the Madrid sky on fire. As night falls, the Royal Palace is theatrically silhouetted against the stars. *See p 17.*

❹ Getting lost in Habsburg Madrid. History oozes from every

Enjoy a lazy day in the Retiro Gardens.

stone in the heart of Habsburg Madrid. The web of narrow streets and enchanting squares around the showcase Plaza Mayor has changed little since the 16th century. *See p 35.*

❺ Sipping cocktails at a hip rooftop bar. Once the heat of summer kicks in, everyone flocks to the *terrazas* (outdoor bars). Best of these are the fashionable rooftop bars at some of the city's hottest hotels, including the Penthouse at the übercool Me Madrid (p 141), and La Terraza at every fashionista's favorite, the Hotel Urban (p 141). Dressing up, relaxing with a cocktail, and watching the city sparkle down below is one of my favorite Madrid experiences.

❻ Gazing at the masterworks of the Paseo del Arte. Madrid's three great art museums—the Prado, the Thyssen, and the Reina Sofía—are among the finest anywhere in the world. From the Italian primitives in the Thyssen or the masterpieces by Velázquez in the Prado, to the latest contemporary creations at the Reina Sofía, the capital has it all. *See p 29.*

❼ Choosing gourmet goodies at the Mercado de San Miguel. This beautifully restored 19th-century glass-and-iron market has become a mecca for gourmets. It is a great place to pick up local hams and cheeses, and even to sample some of them at one of the counter bars. *See p 70.*

❽ Tapas-bar hopping. Madrid's tapas bars range from spit-and-sawdust dives that have barely changed in decades to swish gourmet establishments serving fashionable wines and elegant nibbles. Eating and drinking your way around the city is an utter joy. *See p 11.*

⑨ Rummaging for bargains in the Rastro. I am a flea market addict, and few can compare with Madrid's Rastro for sheer scale and exuberance. The range is astonishing—from traditional leather goods to car parts. The post-Rastro crawl around the tapas bars of La Latina is just as much fun as exploring the market itself. *See p 67.*

⑩ Strolling among the bookstalls on the Cuesta de Moyano. The Cuesta de Moyano is Madrid's answer to the Bouquinistes of Paris, and one of my favorite places to while away a lazy afternoon. Along one side of this shaded, pedestrianized street, there are wooden kiosks

piled high with books, with more sold from trestle tables along the middle. *See p 31.*

⑪ Joining in a popular street festival. During the summer, the city explodes with a series of colorful, traditional festivals, which take place in various neighborhoods, usually in honor of the patron saint, San Isidro. The biggest are the Fiestas de San Isidro in May, but each festival offers visitors a chance to join in with traditional events, from parades to street parties. *See p 160.*

⑫ Exploring the ancient streets of historic Toledo. I really enjoy escaping to the beautiful old city of Toledo, losing myself in its lovely streets and quiet corners. It's much more enjoyable to stay the night, when the city empties of day-trippers. *See p 156.* ●

Fans for sale at Rastro Market.

The Best **in One Day**

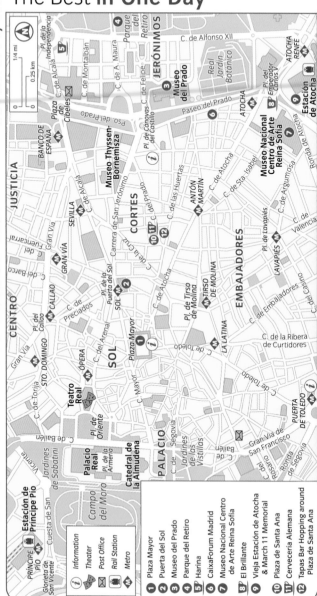

1/4 mi
0.25 km

Parque del Retiro

JERÓNIMOS

C. de Alfonso XII

Real Jardín Botánico

Museo del Prado

ATOCHA RENFE

Plaza de Cibeles

Pso. del Prado

Paseo del Prado

Estación de Atocha

Pl. del Emperador Carlos V

BANCO DE ESPAÑA

Museo Thyssen-Bornemisza

Museo Nacional Centro de Arte Reina Sofía

JUSTICIA

CORTES

C. de las Huertas

ANTÓN MARTÍN

EMBAJADORES

LAVAPIÉS

C. de Valencia

SEVILLA

Gran Vía

CALLAO

CENTRO

Pl. del Callao

STO. DOMINGO

ÓPERA

SOL

Pl. de la Puerta del Sol

Plaza Mayor

Pl. de Tirso de Molina

LA LATINA

TIRSO DE MOLINA

Teatro Real

Pl. de Oriente

PALACIO

Palacio Real

Catedral de la Almudena

PRÍNCIPE PÍO

Estación de Príncipe Pío

Campo del Moro

Jardines de Sabatini

Glorieta de San Vicente

PUERTA DE TOLEDO

Gran Vía de San Francisco

Ronda de Segovia

	Information
	Theater
	Post Office
	Rail Station
	Metro

1. Plaza Mayor
2. Puerta del Sol
3. Museo del Prado
4. Parque del Retiro
5. Harina
6. CaixaForum Madrid
7. Museo Nacional Centro de Arte Reina Sofía
8. El Brillante
9. Vieja Estación de Atocha & March 11 Memorial
10. Plaza de Santa Ana
11. Cervecería Alemana
12. Tapas Bar Hopping around Plaza de Santa Ana

Previous page: Palacio Real.

This tour takes in some of the finest achievements of the Habsburg kings, from their showcase square, the Plaza Mayor, to their world-class art collection in the Prado. For contrast, check out the superb contemporary art in the Reina Sofía, but make time for a breather in the glorious Parque del Retiro. Finish up with some tapas-bar hopping around the Plaza de Santa Ana. START: **Metro to Sol.**

1 ★★★ Plaza Mayor. This has been the center of the city since long before Madrid became capital, but it was the Habsburg kings who ordered the transformation of the ancient market place into the spectacular set piece that it is today. A huge, rectangular square flanked on all sides by symmetrical mansions with graceful porticoes, the Plaza Mayor has been the stage for hangings, bullfights, and royal ceremonies since the late 16th century. Order a coffee from one of the cafes with outdoor tables and soak up the history. *See also p 39.* ⏱ *45 min. Metro: Sol.*

2 ★ Puerta del Sol. You will no doubt find yourself at the Puerta del Sol several times during your visit, however briefly. It's the city's main transportation hub, and the confluence of numerous metro and bus routes. Once this was one of the most

Soak up the history at Plaza Mayor.

piquant squares in the city, where anything and anyone was available for a price. Nowadays it's worth a quick visit to check out **Kilómetro Cero**—the very center of Spain, which is marked on a plaque in front of the **Casa de Correos** (the ocher-colored 18th-century building bristling with flags). If you're in Madrid on New Year's Eve, this is the place to come, armed with a bottle of *cava* and 12 grapes (one for each chime during the countdown to midnight). ⏱ *20 min. Metro: Sol.*

3 ★★★ Museo del Prado. This is one of the world's greatest art museums, originally assembled by the Habsburg kings. To see it properly would take days, so pick up a floor plan and select specific galleries according to your interests. The Prado has an unsurpassed collection of Spanish art, particularly works by the greatest artist of the Spanish Golden Age, **Diego Velázquez** (1599–1660). The museum's grandest gallery, the huge octagonal Room 12 (in the main Villanueva building), contains some of his masterworks. The undisputed star of the collection hangs here: *Las Meninas* (1656) depicts the 4-year-old Infanta Margarita and her entourage, with Velázquez himself gazing out from behind his easel. Look beyond the apparently simple court scene, and its complexity and elusiveness grows. Don't miss the works of **Francisco de Goya** (1746–1828), court painter to Carlos III and Carlos IV. The most famous of his paintings in the Prado's collection include the sensuous *Nude Maja* (ca. 1800) and its counterpart

King Carlos III in Puerta del Sol.

The Clothed Maja (ca. 1803), which hang side by side in Gallery 36. (Eighteenth-century aristocrats liked to dress up in the folk costumes of "Majos" and "Majas"—the capital's famously flamboyant working-class men and women.) For some contrast, head to Galleries 66 and 67 to see the "Black Paintings," a series of dark and disturbing murals painted during Goya's last years. Take a peek at the cloister before you leave, to see how cleverly Rafael Moneo managed to incorporate the 16th-century Gothic arches and columns into his elegant 2007 extension. ⏲ *2 hr. See tour p 31.*

④ ★★★ kids **Parque del Retiro.** After the fascinating but overwhelming Prado, take refuge in the nearby Retiro Park. Kids can let off steam in the playgrounds by the Calle Alcalá entrance or kick a ball around the lawns. The elegantly arranged Parterre gardens are restful, while the enormous Estanque (lake) with its marble colonnade hints that it was once a royal garden (attached to the long-demolished palace of Buen Retiro). Now teeming with carp, the lake is filled with wooden boats that can be rented by the hour. The atmosphere is carnivalesque, with mime artists, buskers, ice-cream vendors, and snack kiosks. The Retiro is a great place for a picnic, and, even on the hottest day, you can always find a shady corner. My favorite spot is by the pool near the beautiful Palacio de Cristal. ⏲ *1 hr. See also p 95.*

⑤ ★ **Harina.** There are kiosks in the park for a quick bite, but this chic, white-painted bakery-cum-cafe by the Puerta de Alcalá serves tasty soups, sandwiches, salads, and cakes. Eat in or take out. *Plaza de la Independencia 6–8.* ☎ *91-522-87-85. www.harinamadrid.com. Coffee and a pastry 3.50€.*

Museo del Prado is one of the world's greatest art museums.

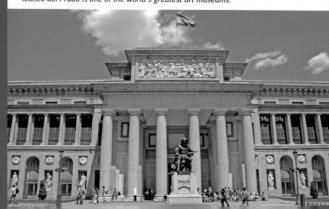

Discount Museum Passes

With a single ticket, the Abono Paseo del Arte, costing 17.60€, you can visit the Prado, the Thyssen-Bornemisza, and the Reina Sofía. Buy it at museum ticket desks or the tourist office (p 33).

The **Madrid Card,** available for 24, 48, or 72 hours, offers admission to more than 40 museums (including the Paseo del Arte museums), and major attractions including the zoo, funfair, and Bernabéu soccer stadium. It costs 32€, 42€, or 52€, respectively, or 38€, 52€, or 65€ with unlimited use of the public transportation system. It's only worth the investment if you intend to sightsee very intensively. Another option includes unlimited use of the sightseeing bus; 1-day cards cost 41€ and 2-day cards cost 49.50€. A simpler version, offering admission to only two museums, costs 22€. For more information see www.madridcard.com.

6 ★★ kids **CaixaForum Madrid.** The CaixaForum, which opened in 2007, is a dynamic arts center that occupies a spectacularly transformed 19th-century power station. It's topped with a two-floor annex enclosed by a bold rusted iron sculpture, and contains a great cafe-restaurant and bookstore. Get a program in advance from the tourist office: All kinds of activities are on offer, from art exhibitions and concerts to special activities for children. Best of all is the **Vertical Garden,** by French botanic artist Patrick Blanc, an enormous wall covered with more than 200 plant species in intricate designs. It's my favorite piece of public art in the city. ⏲ *1 hr. Paseo del Prado 36.* ☎ *91-330-73-00. www.lacaixa.es/ obrasocial. Admission varies according to exhibition and* activity, but most are free. *Tues–Sun 10am–8pm. Closed Mon. Metro: Atocha.*

7 ★★★ **Museo Nacional Centro de Arte Reina Sofía.** The fashionable Reina Sofía is the city's modern art museum. If time is very tight, head straight to gallery 7 to see Picasso's masterpiece, *Guernica* (1937). It was painted in memory of the 1937 bombing by the Germans of an ancient Basque town—a brutal act that happened with Franco's approval. It was painted for the Spanish Pavilion at the Paris World's Fair of 1937. The surrounding galleries put *Guernica* in context by displaying other artworks (including a beautiful Calder mobile) that shared the 1937 Pavilion, as well as stark images from the Spanish Civil War, including Robert Capa's photographs. ⏲ *1 hr. See also p 32,* **11**.

Parque del Retiro sculpture.

CaixaForum, the city's newest art institution.

8 ★ **El Brillante.** There's a stylish cafe in the Reina Sofía, but for more traditional fare head to El Brillante. It's been serving enormous calamari sandwiches for 50 years. *C/ Argumosa 43.* ☎ *91-467-02-02. Sandwiches 3.50€–5.50€.*

Museo Nacional Centro de Arte Reina Sofía.

9 ★ **Vieja Estación de Atocha & March 11 Memorial.** It might seem strange to suggest visiting a train station, but this must be the only one in the world to offer an indoor tropical palm forest, complete with tiny turtles in pools. It's just across the street from the Reina Sofía museum, and is a great place to warm up on icy winter days. On a more somber note, this station was the scene of a bomb attack on March 11, 2004: The 192 victims are remembered in a luminous crystal monument etched with the condolence messages delivered in the wake of the attack. ⏱ *30 min. Metro: Atocha.*

10 ★ **kids Plaza de Santa Ana.** It's an easy stroll up from Atocha to the Plaza de Santa Ana, the main hub of the **Barrio de las Letras** (p 57), and old stomping ground of writers such as Cervantes, Quevado, and Lope de Vega, and more recently, Ernest Hemingway and Nobel-prize-winning writer Jacinto Benavente. The square is crammed on every side with great cafes, bars, and restaurants, all overlooked at one end by the very stylish **Me Madrid hotel** (p 141), which occupies a turn-of-the-20th-century wedding cake of a building, and at the other by the neoclassical **Teatro Español** (p 58), which stands on the site of one of the city's first purpose-built theaters. There are numerous terraces to sit outside and enjoy a beer, while the kids are kept happy with a couple of play areas. I avoid the square at weekends, when it gets too crowded, and enjoy it best early in the evening during the week. ⏱ *1 hr.* *Metro: Sol.*

Fresh seafood at Hemingway's old haunt, the Alemana.

11 ★ **Cerveceria Alemana.** Yet another of Hemingway's haunts, this celebrated tavern retains its original wooden facade, draped lace curtains, and scuttling, long-aproned waiters. Traditional tapas such as croquetas, tortilla, and fried fish are accompanied by a wide range of beers. I like it best in winter, when the wood-paneled bar feels especially cozy. *Plaza de Santa Ana.* ☎ *91-429-70-33. Beer and a tapa 4.50€.*

12 ★★ **Tapas Bar Hopping around Plaza de Santa Ana.** The streets around the Plaza de Santa Ana are crammed with bars, cafes, and clubs, making it one of the most popular nightlife zones in the city. A good bar option is **Naturbier** (www.naturbier.com) at No. 9. Later on, try the delightfully eccentric cafe-bar **El Imperfecto** (p 117), and finish the night at the laidback jazz bar, **Populart** (p 126). *Metro: Sol.*

There are many terrace cafes on Plaza de Santa Ana.

The Best **in Two Days**

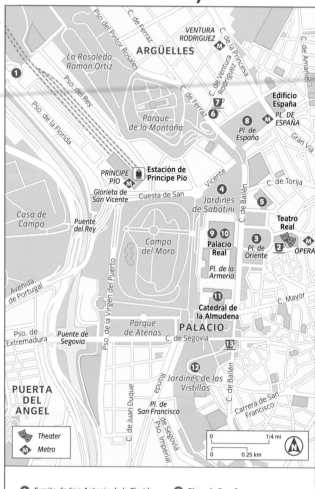

1 Ermita de San Antonio de la Florida

2 Café de Oriente

3 Plaza de Oriente

4 Jardines de Sabatini

5 Monasterio de la Encarnación

6 Museo Cerralbo

7 Cáscaras

8 Plaza de España

9 Palacio Real

10 Galeria de Pinturas

11 Catedral de la Almudena

12 Jardines de las Vistillas

13 Restaurante El Ventorrillo

This tour offers a little bit of everything: Aristocratic mansions and royal palaces, lavish squares, an art-filled convent, a panoramic dome, the tomb of that most Madrileño of painters, Goya, and secret gardens where you can catch your breath. End the day with a cocktail and watch the sun slip over the Guadarrama mountains. START: **Metro Príncipe Pío (one stop on line R from Ópera).**

1 ★★ **Ermita de San Antonio de la Florida.** A neoclassical jewel, this small chapel is now most famous for its vivid frescoes, painted by one of Spain's most outstanding artists, **Francisco de Goya** (1746–1828). Goya died in Bordeaux, France, but his remains were brought back to this chapel in 1919. The frescoes fill the entire cupola and glow with life and color. They depict St. Anthony raising a murdered man to life in order to exonerate the saint's father, who stood accused of the crime. Instead of a heavenly host surrounding the saint, Goya painted in a balcony and filled it with contemporary Madrileños, particularly the *majos* and *majas* (the swaggering dandies of the working class), who were his favorite subject. The painting is transformed from a dull religious work into an engaging evocation of the city. Visit around June 13, when the chapel is the center of a lively street festival in honor of the

saint. 🕐 *45 min. Glorieta de San Antonio de la Florida 5.* ☎ *91-542-07-22. www.munimadrid.es/ermita. Free admission. Sept–July Tues–Fri 9:30am–8pm, Sat–Sun 10am–2pm; Aug Tues–Fri 9:30am–2:30pm, Sat–Sun 10am–2pm. Closed Mon, Jan 1, May 1, Sept 9, Dec 24, Dec 25, Dec 31. Metro: Príncipe Pío.*

2 ★★ **Café de Oriente.** This may be one of the more touristy cafes, but it's still one of the best. Its gilded salons are popular with well-heeled ladies and their lapdogs, but the fantastic terrace overlooking Madrid's most regal square is the place to sit. Perfect for a leisurely breakfast while you admire the views of the gardens, fountains, and the splendid Royal Palace. *Plaza de Oriente 2.* ☎ *91-541-39-74. www.cafede oriente.es. Coffee and a pastry 4€.*

Take a stroll around the grand Plaza de Oriente.

Jump on the efficient metro at Atocha, with a quick change at Sol, to emerge at Ópera.

❸ ★★ kids Plaza de Oriente. Walk around to the front of the lavish Opera House to find the impressive Plaza de Oriente. Flanked by the enormous Royal Palace on one side and the Opera House on the other, it is filled with manicured gardens, fountains, and statues. After a short stroll around the gardens (there's a playground for youngsters), treat yourself to an ice cream and grandstand views at one of the smart cafe terraces. ⏲ *20 min. Metro: Ópera.*

❹ Jardínes de Sabatini. King Juan Carlos I opened these gardens to the public in 1978. They are named after the 18th-century Italian architect Francesco Sabatini, who designed the stables that originally occupied the spot. Laid out in the 1930s, they are now a restful retreat, shaded with trees and adorned with classical sculptures of Spanish kings. The gardens offer beautiful views of the Royal Palace. ⏲ *20 min. C/ Bailén 15. Metro: Ópera.*

❺ ★★ kids Monasterio de la Encarnación. This austere, beautiful convent was established in 1611 by Margarita of Austria, wife of

Felipe III. It is still home to a closed community of nuns, but visits are possible with a guide. Most of its treasures, acquired thanks to its royal patron, have long been dispersed, but the lack of adornment only highlights the restrained elegance of the baroque building. The star attraction is the relic room, a thrillingly macabre chamber lined with more than 4,000 reliquaries containing the bones, hair, teeth, and limbs of saints and martyrs. Foremost among them is the blood of San Pantaleón, said to liquefy every year on July 27. If it happens at any other time, so legend goes, the city is in danger. ⏲ *1 hr. Plaza de la Encarnación 1.* ☎ *91-454-88-00. www.patrimonionacional.es. Adults 3.60€, 2.90€ students and children 5–16, free Wed for E.U. citizens; combined admission ticket with Monasterio de Las Descalzas Reales (p 37, ❿) adults 6€, 4.90€ students and children 5–16. Guided tours run approximately every 45 min Tues, Wed, Thurs, Sat 10:30am–12:45pm and 4–5:45pm, Fri 10:30am–12:45pm, Sun and public hols 11am–1:45pm. Closed Jan 1, Easter weekend, May 1, May 15, Sept 9, Dec 24, Dec 25, Dec 31. Metro: Ópera.*

Jardínes de Sabatini.

Monasterio de la Encarnación.

6 ★★ Museo Cerralbo. This sumptuous mansion was built between 1883 and 1893 for the 17th Marqués de Cerralbo, a wealthy Spanish politician, archaeologist, and collector. He gathered more than 50,000 artworks—including paintings, sculpture, crystal, porcelain, coins, engravings, tapestries, armor, and clocks—which are beautifully displayed in the gorgeous salons. Although the gilded ballroom and reception rooms are dazzling, I prefer the quieter, more intimate, charms of the private family rooms. Look out for a 19th-century Ericsson telephone in the Red Room. 🕐 *1 hr. C/ Ventura Rodríguez 17.* ☎ *91-547-36-46. http:// museocerralbo.mcu.es. Admission 3€ adults, free for students, under-18s, and on Sun. Tues–Wed, Fri–Sat 9:30am–3pm, Thurs 9:30am–3pm, 5–8pm, Sun and public hols Sun 10am–3pm. Closed Mon, Jan 1, Jan 6, May 1, Nov 9, Dec 24, Dec 25, Dec 31. Metro: Ventura Rodríguez or Plaza de España.*

7 kids Cáscaras. A colorful, modern restaurant that specializes in tortillas (Spanish omelets), but also serves a good range of salads, grilled meats, and veggie options. Good value. *C/ Ventura Rodríguez 7.* ☎ *91-542-83-36. www.restaurante cascaras.com. Dishes 4.50€–9€.*

8 Plaza de España. This large square was laid out at the height of the Franco era, and is surrounded by monolithic office blocks. Otherwise unimpressive, the square is worth a visit for the flamboyant fountain at the center, where bronze statues of Cervantes' comic heroes, *Don Quijote* and Sancho Panza, look on their way to tilt at windmills. 🕐 *15 min. Metro: de España.*

9 ★★★ kids Palacio Real. Prepare yourself for an assault on the Royal Palace, an immense 18th-century construction that has almost 3,000 rooms. This is still the official residence of the Spanish king, Juan Carlos I, although his family usually resides at the smaller Palacio de la

The Museo de las Colecciones Reales (Museum of the Royal Collections)

It's hard to miss the huge hoardings sitting between the Royal Palace and the Cathedral on the Plaza de la Armería. Behind them, the city's biggest new museum is being constructed. When it opens in 2014 or 2015, it will hold a vast collection of Royal treasures, not least the magnificently gilded ceremonial carriages. A single room will be dedicated to tapestries, with between 80 and 130 precious objects taken from the royal holdings (which currently number over 3,000). All told, it is expected that the museum will exhibit more than 150,000 objects, of which approximately half have never before been on public display.

Zarzuela in Madrid's northern suburbs, and the palace is used mainly for ceremonial events. Perhaps fortunately, just a handful of rooms are open to the public. As well as the lavish salons of the main palace, the complex includes a pair of smaller museums and a picture gallery (Galería de Pinturas, ⑩, below). For highlights of the palace interior, see p 35. Reached from the vast Plaza de la Armería in front of the palace are the two smaller museums: A charming 17th-century pharmacy, complete with porcelain jars and wooden cabinets; and the Royal Armory, with extravagant suits of armor for men and mounts. Look for the engraved armor used by indefatigable conqueror Charles V (Carlos I of Spain) in the Battle of Mühlberg (1547). ⏲ *1½ hr.* *C/ Bailén.* ☎ *91-454-87-00. Admission to Palace, Picture Gallery (see below), Pharmacy, and Royal Armory: 10€ adults, 5€ students and children 5–16; guide 7€, audioguide 4€. Free for E.U. citizens (take your passport) Wed–Thurs 3–6pm (Oct–Mar), 5–8pm (Apr–Sept). Oct–Mar Mon–Sat 10am–6pm, Sun 10am–4pm; Apr–Sept Mon–Sat 10am–8pm, Sun 10am–4pm. Closed Jan 1, Jan 7,* *May 1, Sept 9, Oct 12, Dec 24, Dec 25, Dec 31. Metro: Ópera.*

⑩ ★ **Galería de Pinturas (Picture Gallery).** If you don't have time to visit the entire palace complex, a visit to the painting gallery will give you a good introduction. The gallery is housed in the restored 19th-century apartments of the Infanta Isabel Francisca, and contains works by Caravaggio,

Catedral de la Almudena.

The immense 18th-century Palacio Real.

Velázquez, and Flemish masters. Complementing the paintings is a collection of historic musical instruments (including a 17th-century double bass) and some exquisitely embroidered linen and textiles. It's impossible not to wonder how a delicate princess could sleep under the weight of a gold and brocade bed cover. 🕐 *1hr. See also* 🕘*, above.*

🕚 ★ **Catedral de la Almudena.** Facing the Royal Palace is the massive cathedral, completed in 1993. Peep in to see the contemporary murals and stained glass windows, and head down to the crypt to find the statue of La Virgen de la Almudena, the city's patron saint, who is credited with ousting the Moors during the Reconquest. The museum contains lavish liturgical robes and church plate, but the highlight is the climb to the cupola for stunning views over Madrid's skyline. 🕐 *45 min. Plaza de la Almudena s/n.* ☎ *91-542-22-00. Admission 6€. Mon–Sat 10am– 2:30pm. Metro: Ópera.*

🕛 ★★ **Jardínes de las Vistillas.** These small gardens, unfortunately rather shabby, are at the center of a buzzing bar and restaurant district, which has sprung up because of the glorious views of the distant sierras. Ignore the gardens and head for the bars and their terraces. The district faces west, and the sight of the setting sun turning the sky scarlet behind the grand silhouettes of the cathedral and Royal Palace is breathtaking. 🕐 *45 min. Metro: La Latina.*

🕐 ★★ **Restaurante El Ventorrillo.** Pull up a chair on the terrace of this old-fashioned restaurant and join the Madrileños watching the sunset. The restaurant has good house wines, beers, and a wide range of tapas. The main dishes are slightly pricey but the setting is unforgettable. *C/ Bailén 14.* ☎ *91-366-35-78. Tapas 4€–25€.*

The Best **in Three Days**

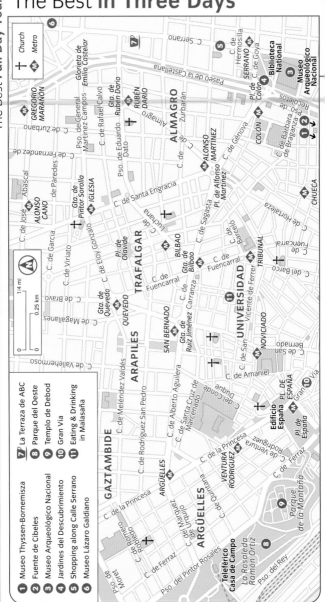

1 Museo Thyssen-Bornemisza
2 Fuente de Cibeles
3 Museo Arqueológico Nacional
4 Jardines del Descubrimiento
5 Shopping along Calle Serrano
6 Museo Lázaro Galdiano
7 La Terraza de ABC
8 Parque del Oeste
9 Templo de Debod
10 Gran Via
11 Eating & Drinking in Malasaña

+ Church
◈ Metro

0   1/4 mi
0   0.25 km

On your third day, while away a morning with the Impressionists and ancient archaeological treasures of two fine museums, then sample the shopping in the chi-chi Salamanca neighborhood. Following an afternoon relaxing in the park, take in the bright lights of the Gran Vía, Madrid's answer to Broadway, and then spend the evening in lively Malasaña. START: **Metro to Serrano.**

❶ ★★★ Museo Thyssen-Bornemisza.

The elegant, neoclassical Palacio de Villahermosa is now home to the vast Thyssen-Bornemisza collection, acquired by the Baron Van Thyssen and his ex-Miss Spain wife, Carmen Cervera. There are more than a thousand artworks, spanning more than 7 centuries, encompassing many of the most important art movements. Given how well the Prado and the Reina Sofía cover Spanish painting and contemporary art, consider concentrating on the Thyssen's unique strengths, particularly a collection of Impressionist and post-Impressionist art that is unrivaled in Spain. Some of my favorites are gathered in gallery 32, including Claude Monet's dreamy *Thaw in Vétheuil* (1881) and van Gogh's *Stevedores at Arles* (1888). In the adjoining gallery (33) are Degas' *Swaying Dancer* (1877–79) and Bonnard's portrait of voluptuous *Misia Godebska* (1908). ⏱ *1 hr. See also p 29,* ❺.

❷ ★ Fuente de Cibeles.

One of the city's best-loved symbols is this extravagant baroque fountain, which features an enormous statue of the earth goddess Cibeles (Cybele) in a chariot pulled by a pair of lions. Real Madrid supporters traditionally gather here for a boisterous celebration whenever their team has an important win. The palatial white building that dominates the square behind the statue was the city's main post office until 2007. Look for the elegant gilded letter slots which have survived its conversion into Madrid's City Hall. ⏱ *15 min. Paseo de Cibeles. Metro: Banco de España.*

❸ ★★★ kids Museo Arqueológico Nacional.

Until 2013, Spain's largest and most important archaeological museum is showing only its highlights while major remodeling works are completed. Among the 268 outstanding pieces

Ancient Byzantine-style treasures can be found in the Museo Arqueológico Nacional.

Calle Serrano, the smartest shopping street in town.

C/ Serrano 13. ☎ *91-577-79-12. http://man.mcu.es. Free admission. Tues–Sat 9:30am–8pm, Sun 9:30am–3pm. Closed Mon, Jan 1, Jan 6, May 1, Sept 9, Dec 24, Dec 25, Dec 31. Metro: Serrano.*

④ kids Jardines del Descubrimiento. The Gardens of Discovery, next to the archaeological museum, commemorate Columbus' voyage to the Americas in 1492. Columbus himself gazes down from a tall column in one corner of the square. In summer, the shady groves of olive and pine trees are the perfect retreat. ⏱ *30 min. Entrances on C/ Serrano and Paseo de la Castellana. Metro: Serrano or Colón.*

⑤ ★★ Shopping along Calle Serrano. Calle Serrano is Madrid's answer to London's Bond Street, or New York's Fifth Avenue. The city's fanciest shopping street has branches of all the main international designers, from Spanish luxury goods store **Loewe** (no. 26) to **Gucci** (no. 49), and attracts It-girls and celebrities with oversized sunglasses and undersized dogs. Even if you're on a budget the window-shopping is fun. **Musgo** (no. 18) has an inexpensive and colorful selection of items for the home, accessories, and gifts. For a traditional deli, try **Mantequerias Bravo,** just off Serrano at Calle Ayala

are ancient Iberian sculptures, including the mysterious Dama de Elche, a 4th-century B.C. bust of a woman in an elaborate headdress. Also seek out the Treasure of Guarrazar, a glittering hoard of Byzantine-style crowns and crosses, which date back to the time of the Visigoths. One of my favorite pieces is an 11th-century Islamic astrolabe, one of the oldest ever made, which belonged to a Toledan mathematician during the time of the Taifas. Kids will be delighted by the enormous dinosaur bones, including a gigantic sauropod femur. ⏱ *1 hr.*

Visit Lázaro Galdiano's varied art collection.

The Templo de Debod originally stood on the banks of the Nile.

24 (☎ 91-575-80-72; www.bravo1931. com). One-stop shoppers should head to the dependable Spanish department store **El Corte Inglés** (p 79), or the plush **ABC Serrano** mall, in an attractively tiled former newspaper office (no. 61). ⏱ *1 hr. C/ Serrano. Metro: Serrano or Retiro.*

6 ★★ **Museo Lázaro Galdiano.** One of the city's most engaging museums, this occupies a handsome neo-Renaissance mansion set within an enclosed garden. Lázaro Galdiano, a wealthy financier, acquired an extraordinary art collection before his death in 1947. Although paintings, including masterpieces by Velázquez, Zurbarán, and Goya, form the core of the collection, they are complemented by an enjoyably eclectic selection of sculpture, ceramics, coins, furniture, textiles, and clocks. The Cámara del Tesoro (Treasure Chamber) contains a curious assortment of reliquaries and antique glassware. Don't forget to take a ride in the antique lift with its velvet seats. ⏱ *1 hr. C/ Serrano 122.* ☎ *91-561-60-84. www.flg.es. Adults 4€, 2€ senior citizens and students, free 11 and under accompanied by adult. Free admission Sun. Wed–Mon 10am–4:30pm. Closed Tues, public hols. Metro: Rubén Darío.*

7 ★ **La Terraza de ABC.** The rooftop cafe-restaurant in the upscale ABC mall comes as a delightful surprise. Splash out on the set lunch menu at the restaurant, or pick up something simpler in the cafe. Get there early, or book ahead, to be sure of a table on the breezy, plant-filled terrace. *C/ Serrano 61.* ☎ *91-575-84-26. www.abcserrano.com. Snacks 5€–12€; set-lunch menu 35€.*

Line 4 of the Metro will whisk you quickly to the Argüelles stop, on the western side of the city. From here, it's a short stroll to:

8 ★★ **kids** **Parque del Oeste.** ⏱ *1 hr. See p 91.*

9 ★★ **kids** **Templo de Debod.** Stroll south through the Parque del Oeste to find the Templo de Debod, which emerges like a mirage from a shallow pool. This 4th-century B.C. Ptolemaic temple was given to the Spanish government in 1968 as a gift for preserving Egyptian monuments threatened by the construction of the Aswan Dam. It originally stood on the banks of the Nile, and a small exhibition inside relates the temple's history. The temple is at its most dramatic at dusk, when it is beautifully reflected in the shimmering pool. ⏱ 1 hr. C/ Ferraz 1. ☎ 91-366-74-15. Free admission. Oct–Mar Tues–Fri 9:45am–1:45pm, 4:15–6:15pm, Sat–Sun 10am–2pm; Apr–Sept Tues–Fri 10am–2pm, 6–8pm, Sat–Sun 10am–2pm. Closed Mon. Free guided visits for families (in Spanish) first Sat of every month (except Aug) at 11:30am and 12:30pm. Metro: Plaza de España.

Hop on an eastbound bus at the Plaza de España (there are more than 20 lines, including 1, 2, 46, 74, 146, and 202) for a run along the:

⑩ ★★ Gran Vía. This is known, with more bravura than truth, as the Broadway Madrileño for its concentration of musical theaters. Laid out in the early 20th century, this long, broad avenue cuts straight across the city, linking east to west. Designed to show the world that Madrid was no backwater sunk in the past, it is lined with outrageously pompous buildings in a mish-mash of once-fashionable styles—lavish neoclassical, sleek Art Deco, and twirling Art Nouveau, all built on a monumental scale. Look up to spot the architectural details, because at street level your gaze is diverted by the shop windows. Every major Spanish chain can be found here, including some great bookstores such as the **Casa del Libro** (p 77), the fashion phenomenon **Zara** (p 81), and plenty more. The Gran Vía is at its best in the early evening, with the sun setting and the neon signs glowing against the buildings. ⏱ 1 hr. Metro: Gran Vía, Callao, or Plaza de España.

⑪ ★ **Eating & Drinking in Malasaña.** From the Gran Vía, stroll up to the Plaza del Dos de Mayo, which is the heart of the lively Malasaña neighborhood. It is ringed by bars and cafes with tables out on the square, and the surrounding streets are packed with plenty more options for eating and drinking. Malasaña has gentrified rapidly in recent years, but has retained plenty of its old-fashioned appeal. Mom-and-pop-style shops sit cheek-by-jowl with designer restaurants, and quirky boutiques rub shoulders with century-old cafes. Among my favorites in the neighborhood are the cafe-bar **Pepe Botella,** C/ San Andrés 9 (☎ 91-522-43-09), the vegetarian restaurant **Isla del Tesoro** (p 107), and the ultra-stylish eatery **Be Chic Loft** (p 102). ●

Gran Vía, linking the city from east to west.

The Highlights of the Prado

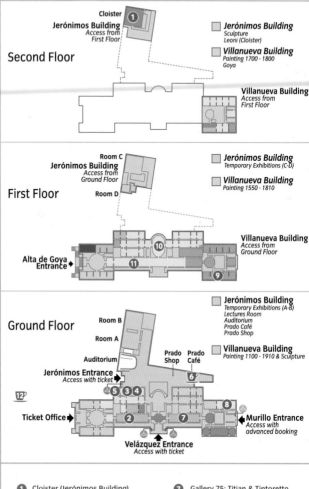

Second Floor

Cloister ①

Jerónimos Building
Access from
First Floor

☐ **Jerónimos Building**
Sculpture
Leoni (Cloister)

☐ **Villanueva Building**
Painting 1700 - 1800
Goya

Villanueva Building
Access from
First Floor

First Floor

Room C

Jerónimos Building
Access from
Ground Floor

Room D

☐ **Jerónimos Building**
Temporary Exhibitions (C-D)

☐ **Villanueva Building**
Painting 1550 - 1810

Villanueva Building
Access from
Ground Floor

Alta de Goya
Entrance ➤

⑩
⑪
⑨

Ground Floor

Room B

Room A

Auditorium

Jerónimos Entrance
Access with ticket ➤

Prado Prado
Shop Café

☐ **Jerónimos Building**
Temporary Exhibitions (A-B)
Lectures Room
Auditorium
Prado Café
Prado Shop

☐ **Villanueva Building**
Painting 1100 - 1910 & Sculpture

⑫

Ticket Office ➤

⑤ ③ ④
②
⑦
⑥
⑧

➤ **Murillo Entrance**
Access with
advanced booking

Velázquez Entrance
Access with ticket

---

① Cloister (Jerónimos Building)

② Gallery 49: Fra' Angelico,
   Raphael & Dürer

③ Gallery 56A: Bosch

④ Gallery 56A: Breughel

⑤ Gallery 58: Rogier van der Weyden

⑥ Prado Café

⑦ Gallery 75: Titian & Tintoretto

⑧ Galleries 66 & 67:
   Goya's "Black Paintings"

⑨ Gallery 36: Goya

⑩ Galleries 10–14, 27: Velázquez

⑪ Galleries 26: El Greco

⑫ La Terraza y El Jardín del Ritz

Previous page: Catedral de la Almudena.

The Prado is one of the world's greatest museums, with a rich collection originally gathered by the Habsburg monarchs. The Spanish art is unrivaled, and includes masterpieces by Velázquez and Goya. The following tour takes in my favorite galleries, but covers only a fraction of the entire collection. START: **Metro to Banco de España, then a 5-minute walk. Trip length: 5 hr.**

① ★★ Cloister (Jerónimos Building). The 16th-century cloister belonging to the nearby Jerónimos monastery was incorporated into Rafael Moneo's glassy 2007 extension to the Prado. It's a graceful setting for handsome bronzes depicting Habsburg rulers. ⏱ *15 min.*

② ★★★ Gallery 49: Fra' Angelico, Raphael & Dürer. Fra' Angelico's moving *Annunciation* (1426–27) depicts the Angel announcing Mary's impending conception in a haze of golden light. Raphael's *Portrait of a Cardinal* (ca. 1510) stands out for its masterful realism, from the perfect folds of the crimson silk to the calculation in the cold eyes. Around the same time, Dürer was painting *Adam and Eve* (1507), foregoing any extraneous background detail to focus

attention on his sensuous nudes. ⏱ *30 min.*

③ ★★★ Gallery 56A: Bosch. In Gallery 56A visitors pack themselves around the bizarre, surrealistic visions of the Flemish painter, Hieronymus Bosch. The unsettling *Garden of Earthly Delights* is probably his most famous painting. Divided into three panels, with Paradise on the left, Hell on the right, and the sins of the flesh in the center, it has defied interpretation since it was brought to court in the 16th century. ⏱ *30 min.*

④ ★★★ Gallery 56A: Breughel. I love Pieter Breughel's vibrant, earthy depictions of ordinary people, but his gloomier *Triumph of Death* (1562) gives me the shivers. It shows a desolate landscape in

Museo del Prado.

which dogs pick over the bones of the slaughtered, and was influenced by Bosch, whom Breughel greatly admired. ⏱ *15 min.*

5 ★★★ **Gallery 58: Rogier van der Weyden.** The electrifying *Descent from the Cross* (ca. 1435) is one of van der Weyden's largest works. It doesn't merely depict the moment when Christ's body is brought from the cross, but captures the cataclysmic pain of a mother who has lost her son. ⏱ *15 min.*

6 **Prado Café.** Take a break at this modern cafe near the main entrance. It has all the atmosphere of an airport lounge, but it's the only option inside the museum. *Main entrance hall. Snacks 4€–12€.*

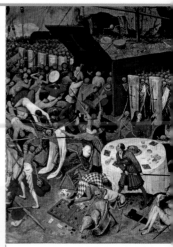

Detail from Breughel's Triumph of Death *(1562).*

7 ★★★ **Gallery 75: Titian & Tintoretto.** The great Venetian painter Titian's portrait of *Charles V at the Battle of Mühlberg* (1548) is considered one of the finest equestrian portraits of all time. Just look at the king's weary expression despite his heroic pose. Titian's equally masterful portrait of *Felipe II With Armor* (1550–51) was sent to Mary Tudor of England during their marriage negotiations. There are also works by another great Venetian colorist, Tintoretto, including the vivid early

The Prado: Practical Matters

Buy tickets, pick up pre-booked tickets, or exchange the Paseo del Arte pass at the ticket offices by the Goya gate at the northern end of the museum. Note that the galleries are sometimes rearranged: Grab a floor plan at the information desk. The museum is at Paseo del Prado s/n (☎ 90-210-70-77; www.museodelprado.es). Admission costs 8€ adults, 4€ students, when bought directly at the ticket office; in advance (by phone or Internet) it's 7€ adults, 4€ students. It's also a leg of the **Paseo del Arte** ticket, which costs 17.60€ (p 29). Admission is free for those 17 and under and for E.U. students under 25, and on Tuesday to Saturday 6pm to 8pm or Sunday 5 to 8pm. General hours are Tuesday to Sunday 9am to 8pm; on December 24, December 31, and January 6, it's open 9am to 2pm, and is closed entirely on Mondays, December 25, January 1, Good Friday, and May 1.

work *Christ Washing the Disciples' Feet* (1547). ⏲ *30 min.*

❽ ★★★ Galleries 66 & 67: Goya's "Black Paintings." Enter the dim galleries that contain Goya's "Black Paintings." In 1819, Goya—by now old, deaf, and sickened by war—moved to a small house outside Madrid, where he painted these bleak and sometimes horrifying murals directly onto the walls of his home. The most famous and graphic is *Saturn Devouring His Son*. ⏲ *30 min.*

❾ ★★★ Gallery 36: Goya. Shake off the gloom with a visit to one of Goya's earlier works: *The Naked Maja* (ca. *1797*). The Inquisition stripped Goya of his position as court painter over this portrayal of a frankly sensual young woman. It's thought that the model was Pepita Tudó, mistress to the Spanish prime minister, Manuel de Godoy. The painting is displayed along with its companion piece, which depicts the same woman fully dressed. ⏲ *20 min.*

❿ ★★★ Galleries 10–14, 27: Velázquez. Gallery 12 is the centerpiece of the entire museum. Here are the finest works by the great Spanish artist Velázquez, including *Las Meninas*, considered one of the greatest paintings of all time (p 32, ⓫). The monumental *Surrender of Breda* (1635) depicts a key moment in Spanish history: the handing over of the keys of the Flemish city of Breda to a Spanish general. In *The Jester Don Diego de Acedo*, Velázquez imbues his subject, one of more than a hundred dwarfs employed at the palace, with a dignity often denied them at court. Adjoining galleries contain Velázquez's royal portraits. ⏲ *1 hr.*

⓫ ★★★ Galleries 26: El Greco. Finish with a shot of the highly charged drama of El Greco. The Crete-born artist trained in Venice and Rome before coming to Spain, where he remained for much of his life, but his art is utterly unlike any of his contemporaries. I like his late *Annunciation* (1596–1606), a swirling, ecstatic moment presided over by a dove. ⏲ *30 min.*

⓬ ★★ La Terraza y El Jardín del Ritz. Next to the Prado, the terrace of the frothy Belle Époque-style Ritz hotel is a refined and relaxing spot for a well-deserved post-Prado cocktail. *Plaza de la Lealtad.* ☎ *91-521-28-57. www.ritz.es. Cocktails 10€–15€.*

Detail from the Surrender of Breda *by Velázquez.*

Highlights of **the Paseo del Arte**

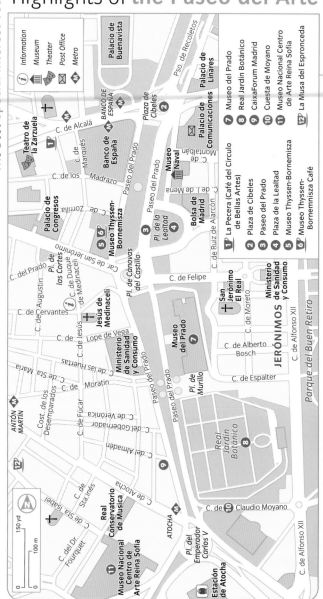

Legend

- ⓘ Information
- 🏛 Museum
- 🎭 Theater
- ⊠ Post Office
- ◈ Metro

1. La Pecera (Café del Círculo de Bellas Artes)
2. Plaza de Cibeles
3. Paseo del Prado
4. Plaza de la Lealtad
5. Museo Thyssen-Bornemisza
6. Museo Thyssen-Bornemisza Café
7. Museo del Prado
8. Real Jardín Botánico
9. CaixaForum Madrid
10. Cuesta de Moyano
11. Museo Nacional Centro de Arte Reina Sofía
12. La Musa del Espronceda

The Paseo del Arte properly refers to Madrid's Big Three museums (the Prado, the Thyssen-Bornemisza, and the Reina Sofía), which are conveniently located within a few minutes' walk of each other. The highlights of the Prado are described on p 25, and below you'll find the best of the Thyssen and the Reina Sofía. START: **Metro to Banco de España. Trip length: 1 day.**

1 ★★ La Pecera (Café del Cir-culo de Bellas Artes). Fortify yourself for a long day's sightseeing beneath the crystal chandeliers of this gorgeous Art Deco cafe. *C/ Alcalá 42.* ☎ *93-360-54-00. Coffee and a pastry 2.50€.*

2 ★ Plaza de Cibeles. The flamboyant statue of the goddess Cibeles (Cybele) in her chariot, surrounded by spurting fountains, has become the city's unofficial symbol. ⏱ *15 min. See also p 19,* **2**.

3 ★ Paseo del Prado. The Paseo del Prado is a relatively short boulevard that runs from the Plaza de Cibeles to the Plaza del Emperador Carlos V in front of Atocha railway station, passing by some of the city's greatest art museums. In the center, a tree-shaded walkway is dotted with benches, fountains, and two children's playgrounds. It was formerly known as the Salón del Prado, where Madrileños would gather in

their finery to flirt and gossip. The ornate carriages have now, unfortunately, given way to the roar of modern traffic. ⏱ *30 min. Metro: Banco de España or Atocha.*

4 ★ Plaza de la Lealtad. A semicircular plaza, just off the Paseo del Prado on the left, contains a tall stone obelisk, set on a monumental plinth within a neat garden. This is the *Monument a Los Caidos por España* (Monument to the Fallen of Spain), erected in the early 19th century in memory of Madrileños shot here by Napoleonic troops on May 2, 1808. In 1985 it was rededicated to all those who have died for Spain. A flame burns perpetually on the monument's steps. Flanking the square is the neoclassical, **Bolsa** (Stock Exchange), with its ranks of splendid columns, and the gorgeous, Belle Époque, Hotel Ritz (p 143). ⏱ *10 min. Metro: Banco de España.*

5 ★★★ Museo Thyssen-Bor-nemisza. Begin with the earliest works, upstairs.

The tree-shaded walkway in the center of Paseo del Prado.

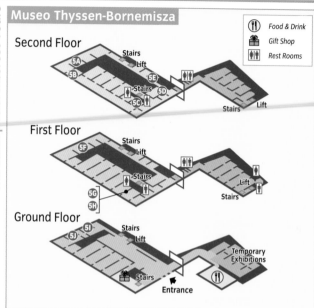

Museo Thyssen-Bornemisza

Food & Drink

Gift Shop

Rest Rooms

Second Floor

Stairs · Lift · Stairs · Stairs · Lift

5A · 5B · 5E · 5D · 5C

First Floor

Stairs · Lift · Stairs · Lift · Stairs

5F · 5G · 5H

Ground Floor

Stairs · Lift · Stairs · Temporary Exhibitions

5I · 5J

Entrance

My favorites here are the miniature **5A van der Weyden's** *Madonna Enthroned* (ca. 1433) and Jan van Eyck's superb diptych of *The Annunciation* (ca. 1435–51) in Room 3. In Room 5, the graceful Renaissance **5B Ghirlandaio's** *Portrait of Giovanna Tornabuoni* (1488) has become the museum's motif. Also note Hans Holbein's iconic *Portrait of King Henry VIII* (ca. 1534–36). In Room 12 **5C Caravaggio's** dramacharged *Saint Catherine of Alexandria* (ca. 1597) heralds the baroque. Head for rooms 16–18 for wonderful Italian landscapes, including **5D Canaletto's** magical depictions of Venice. **5E Rubens'** *Venus and Cupid* (1606–12) is in Room 19. Downstairs, rooms 22–26 include the sweeping skies of **5F Jacob van Ruisdael's** *View of Naarden* (1647). Rooms 32 and 33 are among the best, with a fabulous collection of **5G Impressionist** and **5H post-Impressionist** works, finishing up with harbingers of Cubism such as George Grosz's fiery red *Metropolis* (1916–17). On the entrance level, rooms 41–44 cover from early **5I Cubist** works such as Picasso's *Man with a Clarinet* (1911–12) to Mondrian's extraordinary *New York City, New York* (1940–42). **5J The Synthesis of Modernity** in Galleries 45 and 46 contain Picasso's teasing *Harlequin with a Mirror* (1923), Miró's *Catalan Peasant with a Guitar* (1924), Rothko's *Green on Maroon* (1961), and Jackson Pollocks' *Brown and Silver I* (1951). ⏱ *2 hr. Paseo del Prado 8.* ☎ *91-369-01-51. www.museo thyssen.org. Adults 8€, 5.50€ students, free for 11 and under; temporary exhibition prices vary. Also part of Paseo del Arte ticket (p 29). Tues–Sun 10am–6:30pm. Closed Dec 25, Jan 1, May 1. Metro: Banco de España.*

Museo Thyssen-Bornemisza.

6 ★★ **Museo Thyssen-Bornemisza Café.** Tucked behind the rose garden at the main entrance to this museum is a delightful cafe with a terrace. It's good for a coffee or the fixed-price lunch deal, but steer clear of overpriced sandwiches and salads. *Paseo del Prado.* ☎ 93-302-41-40. *Set lunch 13€, sandwiches 8€–12€.*

7 ★★★ **Museo del Prado.** Continue walking down the Paseo del Prado and you'll see the grand old Prado itself on your left. It deserves a day to itself, so content yourself today with a glance at the columned exterior. *See The Highlights of the Prado, p 25.*

8 ★★ **Real Jardín Botánico.** The perfect antidote to art overload, this glorious 18th-century botanical garden is a verdant haven in the heart of the city. ⏱ *1 hr. See p 85.*

9 ★★ **CaixaForum Madrid.** Admire the striking, contemporary facade and the Vertical Garden as you stroll past the CaixaForum, one of Madrid's newest and most exciting art institutions. *See also p 9,* **6**.

10 ★ **Cuesta de Moyano.** The pedestrianized Calle Claudio Moyano, better known to generations of Madrileños simply as *La Cuesta de Moyano*, makes for an attractive little detour off the Paseo del Arte. Lined with painted wooden kiosks, each with a neat yellow awning, it has been famous for its second-hand book market for almost a century. Refurbished in 2007, the street is now lined with trees and adorned at either end by a statue: A classic 19th-century bronze of the eponymous Claudio Moyano, a Spanish politician at the top

Real Jardín Botánico.

CaixaForum's Vertical Garden.

end, and a homage to Pío Baroja, a turn-of-the-20th-century novelist and philosopher, near the junction with the Paseo del Arte. 🕐 **20 min. Daily 9am–7pm, some stalls close for lunch, others close Sun.**

⓫ ★★★ Museo Nacional Centro de Arte Reina Sofía. The fabulous Reina Sofía museum houses an outstanding contemporary art collection. The biggest draw in the museum, and possibly the most famous artwork in the city (besides the Prado's *Las Meninas*), is Picasso's moving *Guernica* (Room 206; see also p 27, ⓾). The nearby galleries put *Guernica* into context, with other artworks created, like *Guernica*, for the Spanish Pavilion in Paris' International Exhibition of 1937. But some of the greatest Spanish artists of the 20th century are also represented here: The highly personal abstraction of Joan Miró (rooms 206/7); Salvador Dalí's nightmarish, Surrealist works (205); and Juan Gris' influential Cubist paintings (208). Art from 1945 to 1968 is gathered two floors up. Among my favorite works here are photographs of Spain taken in the 1950s by Brassaï (for *Harper's Bazaar*), which contrast with a grittier series from the same era by

Baron Hans Heinrich Thyssen-Bornemisza

The late billionaire industrialist Baron Hans Heinrich Thyssen-Bornemisza devoted much of his life and wealth to the creation of one of the world's great private art collections. At the urging of his fifth wife, Carmen Cervera (crowned Miss Spain in 1961), he established the Thyssen-Bornemisza museum (see above) in Madrid in 1992, and allowed the Spanish government to purchase most of the collection cheaply a year later. The museum neatly fills the gaps in the Prado, with a fine collection of so-called Italian primitives, early Flemish works, Renaissance and baroque painting, and an excellent array of Impressionists and post-Impressionists.

Special Activities in Madrid's Museums

Madrid's great museums all offer excellent programs of activities, which go beyond temporary exhibitions to include everything from family workshops and lectures to film screenings and concerts. Pick up programs at the start of your stay from the tourist office, or directly from museums. During the hot summer months, several offer late-night opening at least one day a week: These include the Museo Thyssen-Bornemisza, which opens its temporary exhibitions until 11pm Tuesday through Saturday, and the Reina Sofía, which is open until 11pm on Saturday nights during August.

Eugene Smith for *Life* magazine. Look too for the electric blue paintings by French artist Yves Klein in Room 424, and the boxy iron creations by Basque sculptor Jorge Oteiza (407). Star architect Jean Nouvel added a bold new wing in 2005, cementing its status as Madrid's most fashionable museum. ⏱ *2 hr. C/ Santa Isabel 52.* ☎ *91-774-10-00. www.museoreinasofia.es. Adults 6€, 3€ students, free for 11 and under; temporary exhibition prices vary. Also part of Paseo del Arte ticket (p 29). Free admission Sat 2:30–9pm, Sun 10am–2:30pm, May 18, Oct 12, Dec 6. Mon, Wed–Sun*

10am–9pm. Closed Dec 24, Dec 25, Dec 31, Jan 1, Jan 6, May 1, May 15, Sept 7. Guided visits, in Spanish only, Mon and Wed 5pm, Sat 11pm. Metro: Atocha.

12 ★★ **La Musa del Espronceda.** An artsy, relaxed hangout near the Reina Sofía, with a big U-shaped tapas bar serving Basque pintxos (slices of baguette with delectable toppings) plus a dining area where you can tuck into the day's specials. *C/ Santa Isabel 17.* ☎ *91-539-12-84. Pintxos 1.80€–3€, set lunch 10€.*

Museo Nacional Centro de Arte Reina Sofía.

Royal Madrid

1 Café de los Austrias
2 Plaza de Oriente
3 Palacio Real
4 Catedral de la Almudena
5 El Anciano Rey de los Vinos
6 Campo del Moro
7 Monasterio de la Encarnación

8 Teatro Real
9 Chocolatería de San Ginés
10 Real Monasterio de las Descalzas Reales
11 Plaza Mayor
12 Casa María

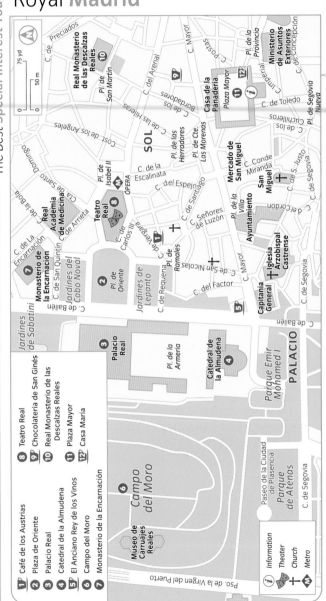

Information
Theater
Church
Metro

Felipe II plucked Madrid from obscurity in 1561 to become Spain's permanent capital, but later monarchs really transformed the city from an overgrown village into a true European metropolis. From the splendid Plaza Mayor to the staggering baroque Royal Palace, this tour takes in the city's greatest Habsburg and Bourbon monuments. START: **Metro to Ópera. Trip length: 1 day.**

1 ★★ Café de los Austrias. One of my favorite cafes, this neighborhood classic has faded mirrors and worn marble columns. Glimpse the Royal Palace from the summer terrace. *Plaza de Ramales 1.* ☎ *91-559-84-36. www.cafedelosaustrias.com. Coffee and a pastry 2.20€.*

2 ★ Plaza de Oriente. With its clipped gardens and fountains, gilded cafes, and views of the Opera House and the Royal Palace, this is a lavish square. ⏲ *20 min. See p 14,* **3**.

3 ★★★ Palacio Real. In 1734, the old Royal Palace (built on the ruins of the Arabic fortress that once occupied this hill) was destroyed in a great fire. The Bourbon monarchs decided to dazzle their new subjects and impress other European monarchs with a spectacular baroque palace. Be thankful that Italian architect

Juvarra's original plans were never carried out: His vision of a palace to vie with Versailles was over three times the size of the current mammoth edifice with its 3,000 rooms. Among the rooms you really shouldn't miss are the extravagant **Throne Room,** with a fresco by the great Venetian painter Tiepolo; the silver-and-gold **Gasparini Room,** used by Carlos III to receive guests; and the **Porcelain Room,** an eye-popping rococo vision encrusted with porcelain made in the royal factory that once stood in the Retiro gardens. Other highlights include the **Hall of Mirrors,** which took its inspiration from Versailles, the 19th-century **Gala Banqueting Hall,** and the musical instruments in the **Stradivarius Room.** The **Painting Gallery** contains some remarkable works by Velázquez, Caravaggio, and Goya. Off the Plaza de la Armería are two more museums:

Explore the extravagant rooms in the Palacio Real.

What a Day for an Auto-de-Fé

The Spanish Inquisition was established by the "Catholic Monarchs," Ferdinand and Isabella, in the late 15th century, but only reached the height of its power in the early 17th century. Felipe II, deeply religious and terrified of heresy, gave the Inquisition far-reaching powers to investigate any diversion from his rigid orthodoxy. Thousands were tried in the public ceremonies known as *auto-de-fé* (which means "act of faith") and those who failed to recant publicly were condemned to a terrible death. In just 1 day in 1680, more than 118 prisoners were tried, of whom 21 were burned alive.

the **Royal Pharmacy** and the **Royal Armory.** I prefer to see the Royal Palace in small doses, and recommend leaving the latter two museums for another day. I also recommend the audioguide over the guided tour: You'll get much the same information but can be more selective in allocating your time. 🕐 2½ hr. See p 15, ⑨.

The neo-baroque Catedral de la Almudena.

④ ★★ **Catedral de la Almudena.** Outside the Royal Palace, the great dome of the Catedral de la Almudena is directly in front of you. Curiously, Madrid had no cathedral until 1993, when this rather dull, neo-baroque construction was finally completed. It is now Spain's most important cathedral, where royal births, christenings, and weddings are celebrated (including Prince Felipe's marriage to Leticia, a glamorous TV journalist, in 2004). Don't miss the rooftop views. 🕐 20 min. See p 17, ⑪.

⑤ ★ **El Anciano Rey de los Vinos.** The century-old El Anciano Rey de los Vinos offers wines, including traditional vermut de grifo (fortified wine from the barrel), to go with the old-fashioned tapas. Perfect for parched palace visitors. *C/ Bailén 19.* ☎ *91-559-53-32. www.elancianoreydelosvinos.es. Tapas 2.50€–10€.*

⑥ ★★ kids **Campo del Moro.** Behind the northern facade of the Royal Palace, just beyond the Plaza de Oriente, are the elegant Sabatini Gardens, a calm oasis after the gilded palace interiors. Beyond them, you can take the Cuesta de

Monasterio de la Encarnación.

San Vicente downhill toward the entrance to the Casa de Campo, the former Royal Gardens that spread down the hill behind the Royal Palace. In the late 19th century, these shaded pathways, flower gardens, pools, and fountains were laid out in the Romantic English style. Quiet, cool, and beautiful, this has spectacular views of the Royal Palace, elegantly framed by sweeping avenues. ⏱ *45 min. Entrances on Paseo Virgen del Puerto and Cuesta de San Vicente.* ☎ *91-454-88-00. Free admission. Oct–Mar Mon-Sat 10am–6pm, Sun 9am–6pm; Apr–Sept Mon–Sat 10am–7pm, Sun 10am– 7pm. Metro: Lago, Batán, or Casa de Campo.*

7 ★★ kids **Monasterio de la Encarnación.** Once you've scrambled back up the hill from the Campo de Moro, make for the Monasterio de la Encarnación, established for royal nuns. ⏱ *1 hr. See p 14,* **5** *.*

8 ★ **Teatro Real.** This lavish opera house was inaugurated in 1850 by Queen Isabella II, and

quickly became one of the most prestigious in Europe. Verdi was present for the Spanish premier of *La Forza del Destino* in 1863, and the Ballets Russes performed in 1925. Tours of the opulent interior are held daily (except Tues), but for the full experience come for an opera (p 127). ⏱ *45 min. Plaza de Isabel II.* ☎ *91-516-06-00. www. teatro-real.com. Adults 5€, free 6 and under. Guided visits Mon, Wed– Fri 10:30am–1pm, Sat–Sun and public hols 11am–1:30pm. Closed Tues. Metro: Ópera.*

9 ★ kids **Chocolatería de San Ginés.** Join locals taking a break from shopping, and dunk the scrumptious *churros* (long, fried dough sticks) into the gloopy hot chocolate for the ultimate afternoon pick-me-up. *C/ Montsió 3.* ☎ *93-302-41-40. Churros and hot chocolate 3€.*

10 ★★ **Real Monasterio de las Descalzas Reales.** This is the finest surviving royal convent, established by Juana of Austria, who was

The Last Spanish Habsburg: Carlos II

Carlos II (1661–1700) suffered such crippling mental and physical infirmities from birth that he was known as "*el Hechizado*"—"the bewitched." The poster child for the perils of inbreeding, his own mother was his father's niece, and the Habsburg royals hadn't married outside the immediate family for more than a century. Carlos II couldn't speak until the age of 4, or walk until the age of 8, and the Habsburg overbite (take a close look at the royal portraits in the Prado) had been magnified to such a degree that he was unable to eat normally or to talk without drooling. Although married twice, he could not father children and his death without issue plunged Spain into the horrors of the Wars of Succession.

widowed at just 19. The original building was erected over the palace in which she was born, and is still home to a small closed community of nuns (you might glimpse them at work in the garden). Thanks to its royal connections, the convent became one of the richest religious institutions in the kingdom, although many of its treasures were later sold during hard times. Some have survived and are described on the (mandatory) guided tour. These tours are officially in Spanish only, but many of the guides are multilingual. The lavish 16th-century staircase, with its wonderful *trompe l'oeil* frescoes (look out for Felipe IV with his family), provides a plush entrance to the convent—and a reminder of the powerful connections enjoyed by the blue-blooded nuns. The lovely cloister, with its peeling frescoes, is the most

Real Monasterio de las Descalzas Reales.

Plaza Mayor.

romantic part of the convent, and I always wish the guide would allow more time to explore the tiny side chapels. The convent is proudest of its fine tapestry collection, designed by Rubens and woven in Brussels. A mirror—supposedly the only one in the convent—allows visitors to see the sketch on the back of the tapestry. There's also a recreation of a spartan cell, complete with scourge to mortify the flesh. ⏱ *1 hr. Plaza de las Descalzas s/n.* ☎ *91-454-88-00. www.patrimonionacional.es. Adults 5€, 4€ students, children 5–16, free Wed to E.U. citizens; combined admission ticket with Real Monasterio de la Encarnación 6€ adults, 4.90€ students and children 5–16. June–Sept Tues–Sat 10am–8pm, Sun 10am–3pm; Oct–May Tues–Thurs, Sat 10:30am–12:45pm and 4–5:45pm. Fri 10:30am–12:45pm, Sun and public hols 11am–1:45pm. Closed Mon, Jan 1, Easter weekend, May 1, May 15, Sept 9, Dec 24, Dec 25, and Dec 31. Metro: Sol.*

⓫ ★★★ **Plaza Mayor.** Completed in 1620, the Plaza Mayor was the magnificent showpiece of the new Habsburg capital. The square could accommodate about a third of the city's total population and became a splendid theater for royal pronouncements, public executions, festivals, and bullfights. The Inquisition's ghastly torture chambers and dungeons were located beneath the square, and the mass trials of heretics, called *autos-de-fé*, were among the most theatrical and terrifying of all the spectacles enacted here (see below). ⏱ *45 min. See also p 7,* ❶. *Metro: Sol.*

⓬ ★ **Casa María.** A modern take on an old-fashioned *casa de comidas* (literally, "eating house," denoting a simple restaurant), Casa María elegantly fuses tradition and modernity in both decor and cuisine. Good set-price lunch menus, a range of tapas, and a terrace on the city's emblematic square. *Plaza Mayor 22.* ☎ *91-369-71-40. Tapas 3€, main dishes 10€.*

Downtown Madrid: The Gran Vía

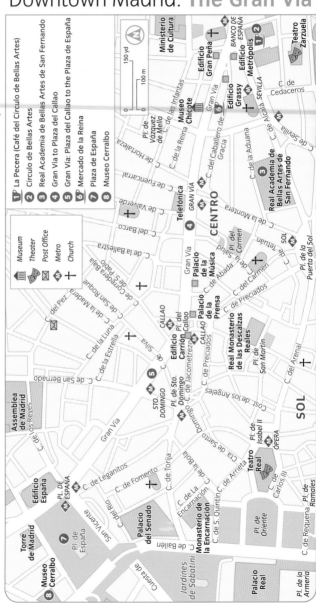

1 La Pecera (Café del Círculo de Bellas Artes)
2 Círculo de Bellas Artes
3 Real Academia de Bellas Artes de San Fernando
4 Gran Vía to Plaza del Callao
5 Gran Vía: Plaza del Callao to the Plaza de España
6 Mercado de la Reina
7 Plaza de España
8 Museo Cerralbo

Museum
Theater
Post Office
Metro
Church

The Gran Vía ("Grand Avenue") sliced through the medieval heart of the city in the early 20th century. Neon lights and thrusting skyscrapers showed the world that Madrid was as bold as New York or any other great metropolis. Some early pizzazz has fizzled, but gaze upward to recapture the jazz-age optimism.

START: **Metro to Banco de España. Trip length: half-day.**

1 ★★ La Pecera (Café del Círculo de Bellas Artes). One of the loveliest Art Deco buildings in the city, now a dynamic art institution (see 2), this contains a fabulously over-the-top cafe for coffee or breakfast. *C/ Alcalá 42. ☎ 93-360-54-00. Breakfast 2.50€–6€.*

2 ★★ Círculo de Bellas Artes. This luscious Art Deco gem, with its billowing curves and enormous picture windows, was originally built as a private club but is now home to a prestigious art institution. Besides the cafe-bar, there is an arthouse cinema, exhibition spaces showing contemporary art and photography exhibitions, a lecture hall, and ballroom. *⏱ 20 min. C/ Alcalá 4. ☎ 91-360-54-00. www.circulobellasartes.com. Metro: Banco de España.*

3 ★★ Real Academia de Bellas Artes de San Fernando. The San Fernando Royal Academy of Fine Arts was established in 1773 and is housed in a restrained baroque palace. Its magnificent art collection is overshadowed by the Prado but is considered one of the finest in Spain. Here you'll find works by Zurbarán, Morales, Goya, Rubens, Caravaggio, and Picasso—and no crowds. *⏱ 1 hr. C/ Alcalá 13. ☎ 91-523-15-99. http://rabasf.insde.es. Adults 3€, 1.50€ students and seniors, free 17 and under; free every Wed, May 18, Oct 12, and Dec 6. Tues–Fri 9am–2pm and 4–7pm, Sat 9am–2:30pm and 4–7pm, Sun–Mon and public hols 9am–2:30pm. Closed Dec 25–26 and Jan 1–6. Metro: Sevilla.*

4 ★★ Gran Vía to Plaza del Callao. The Gran Vía begins where

Art Deco interior of Círculo de Bellas Artes.

"Howitzer Alley"

When Civil War broke out in Spain in 1936, the Republican government, certain that Madrid would fall, fled to safety in Valencia. But against all odds, the city held out, and the famous battle cry of its brave citizens, *"No Pasarán"* ("They shall not pass"), was an inspiration for the entire country. In 1939 Madrid was finally forced to capitulate—the last city in Spain to fall to the Nationalists. During the war years, the Madrileños were under constant attack, and the Gran Vía was nicknamed the Avenida de los Obuses ("Howitzer Alley") or the Avenida del Quince y Medio ("Fifteen and a Half Avenue"), referring to the huge shells that continually rained down. Even now, pockmarks are visible on the Telefónica building, which, as the highest building in the city, came under constant bombardment.

it merges with the Calle Alcalá. This junction is one of the most photographed for its fine ensemble of flamboyant, turn-of-the-20th-century constructions. On the left, the **Edificio Metropolis** (C/ Alcalá 37) is topped with a winged angel; at Gran Vía 1, the **Grassy** building has a neo-Renaissance cupola; opposite, at Gran Vía 2, is the curvaceous **Edificio Gran Peña,** still home to the city's most exclusive gentleman's club. If the Gran Vía doesn't run straight, blame the **Oratorio del Caballero de Gracia** at no. 17: The street was diverted in order to save this graceful 18th-century church from demolition. The white **Telefónica** building, at no. 24, was the first skyscraper in the city, built by an American architect on the Chicago model in the 1920s, and still the 16th tallest building in Madrid. Strolling up the Gran Vía, look out for the Art

The Edificio Metropolis, Gran Vía.

Don Quijote and Sancho Panza, Plaza de España.

Deco **Chicote** cocktail bar, on the right at no. 12. Its walls are still adorned with photos of the rich and famous, from Frank Sinatra to Ava Gardner, who once gathered at this infamous celebrity haunt. ⏱ *45 min. Metro: Banco de España or Callao.*

⑤ ★★ Gran Vía: Plaza del Callao to the Plaza de España. The Art Deco buildings clustered around the **Plaza del Callao** are among my favorites in the whole city. Inspired by the daring new constructions mushrooming in North American cities, many were built as cinemas. Several have survived, and one or two still advertise films with huge, hand-painted billboards. Look out for the gorgeous streamlined curves of the **Edificio Carrión** (Gran Vía 41), which houses the Capitol theater; the **Palacio de la Prensa** (Plaza del Callao 4); and the **Palacio de la Música** (Gran Vía 35). The third stretch of the Gran Vía, up to the Plaza de España, was mostly built after the Civil War, and the mediocrity of the architecture reflects the repressive regime of the era. This stretch is, however, packed with all the best Spanish chain stores, from Zara (p 81) to Mango, offering plenty of great shopping. ⏱ *30 min. Metro: Callao.*

⑥ Mercado de la Reina. Students and local office workers mingle here, attracted by its winning combination of well-priced cuisine and modern design. Try tapas and raciones, or tuck into fresh modern Spanish fare. Unusually, the kitchen is open all day. *Gran Vía 12.* ☎ *91-521-31-98. Tapas 1.30€–5€.*

⑦ ★ Plaza de España. The Plaza de España is a legacy of the Franco era, and none the better for it. It is overlooked by dreary office blocks and a pair of 1950s' skyscrapers, and is redeemed only by the fountain, which includes a bronze statue of Cervantes' great creation *Don Quijote,* with sidekick Sancho Panza. Still, for a clichéd but fun tourist photo, there's nowhere better. ⏱ *30 min.*

⑧ ★★★ Museo Cerralbo. Tucked behind the Plaza de España is this spellbinding museum, a wonderfully eclectic and intimate collection of artworks gathered in a charming 19th-century mansion. It has recently reopened after an expensive and lengthy refurbishment. ⏱ *1 hr. See p 15,* ⑥.

The Best Special-Interest Tours

Madrid's Quirky Museums

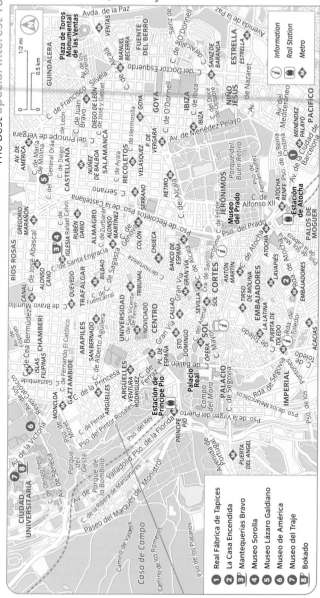

A

0   1/2 mi
0   0.5 km

Information
Rail Station
Metro

1 Real Fábrica de Tapices
2 La Casa Encendida
3 Mantequerías Bravo
4 Museo Sorolla
5 Museo Lázaro Galdiano
6 Museo de América
7 Museo del Traje
8 Bokado

M adrid's trio of outstanding art museums along the Paseo del Arte (p 29) steals the limelight, but there are plenty of curious collections scattered around the city, featuring everything from the extraordinary treasures of South American civilizations to Spanish fashions from the last millennium, as well as tapestries and soccer.

START: **Metro to Menéndez Pelayo. Trip length: 1 day.**

❶ ★★ Real Fábrica de Tapices. I love this museum for the thrill of history it offers. The lavish tapestries are still made on enormous wooden looms, just as they were in the early 18th century when Felipe V founded the factory. Goya's first job in Madrid was creating the elaborate tapestries used to decorate the Royal Palaces. Once there were hundreds of workers; now there is just a handful, but their painstaking labor, threading the bright skeins of wool through the loom, is entrancing. After watching the weavers at their craft, you can take a stroll in the small 18th-century garden. 🕐 *1 hr. C/ Fuentarrabía 2.* ☎ *91-434-05-50. www.realfabricade tapices.com. Adults 4€, 3€ children 6–12, free for 5 and under. Mon–Fri 10am–2pm. Metro: Menéndez Pelayo.*

After a stroll in the garden, hop back on the Metro, and emerge at Atocha.

❷ ★ La Casa Encendida. This cultural foundation focuses on cutting-edge contemporary art, often with a sustainable or green theme: Recent exhibitions have included a comparison of contemporary and ideal cities. The Casa Encendida offers a full program of activities, with everything from film screenings and temporary exhibitions to workshops and family events, and even has its own radio and TV station. The rooftop terrace, with its enticing little garden, is a delight. There's a fair-trade shop inside, with books, gift items, coffee, and chocolate. 🕐 *30 min. Ronda Valencia 2.* ☎ *90-243-03-22. www.lacasa encendida.es. Free admission to most activities but check website. Daily 10am–10pm. Closed public hols. Metro: Atocha.*

Get back on the Metro at Atocha, change at Sol, and get out at Gregorio Marañón.

❸ ★ Mantequerías Bravo. Just a few doors along from the Museo Sorolla (❹), this traditional deli is an ideal spot to pick up the makings of a picnic to enjoy in the museum garden. There are hams, cheeses, olive oils, and a wide selection of Spanish wines. *C/ Ayala 24.* ☎ *91-575-80-72. www.bravo1931.com. Picnic items 3€–10€.*

❹ ★★ Museo Sorolla. The charming 19th-century home of Valencian painter Joaquín Sorolla (1853–1923) is set in a small but

The former home of Valencian painter Joaquín Sorolla.

Museo Lázaro Galdiano.

enchanting garden. Fountains trickle into tiled pools, birds twitter among the greenery, and the little bower is ideal for enjoying a picnic. Inside the house, some of Sorolla's finest Impressionist-style works have been gathered in elegant galleries, and his studio is just as he left it. ⏱ *1 hr. Paseo General Martínez Campos 37.* ☎ *91-310-15-84. http://museo sorolla.mcu.es. Adults 3.50€, free 17 and under and 65 and over; also free Sun, May 18, Oct 12, and Dec 6. Tues–Sat 9:30am–8pm, Sun and public hols 10am–3pm, open until 11:30pm Wed and Thurs from mid-June through late Sept. Closed Mon. Metro: Rubén Darío or Gregorio Marañón.*

The Museo de América houses treasures from the Inca, Mayan, and Aztec cultures.

It's a 15-minute stroll along Paseo General Martínez Campos, crossing Paseo de la Castellana, to reach Calle Serrano and the next stop:

⑤ ★★ Museo Lázaro Galdiano. ⏱ *1 hr. See p 21,* ⑥.

Take the Metro from Nuñez de Balboa to Moncloa, changing at Callao.

⑥ ★ Museo de América. This
large, old-fashioned museum contains treasures from the great Mayan, Inca, and Aztec cultures of the Americas. Few tourists make it here, but there are some interesting artifacts, brought back to Spain by rapacious early explorers of the New World. There are terrifying masks used in war, fine jewelry, painted manuscripts, and mysterious carved stones. ⏱ *45 min. Av. Reyes Católi-cos 6.* ☎ *91-549-26-41. http://museo deamerica.mcu.es. Adults 3€, free 17 and under and 65 and over; also free Sun, May 18, Oct 12, and Dec 6. May–Oct Tues–Sat 9am–8:30pm, Sun and public hols 10am–3pm; Nov–Apr Tues–Sat 9:30am–6:30pm, Sun and public hols 10am–3pm. Closed Mon. Metro: Moncloa.*

Take the steep steps opposite the museum entrance down to the main road, turn right, and next to the traffic circle you'll see:

Real Madrid C.F.

Real Madrid is one of the richest, most successful, and most famous soccer teams in the world. Founded in 1902, the club has won domestic league competition La Liga 31 times, the knockout Copa del Rey 18 times, and the European Cup a record nine times. Tickets for matches at the home stadium, the Estadio Santiago Bernabéu (which has its own Metro stop), are much sought after—particularly when Los Merengues ("the meringues," nicknamed for their white strip) play archrivals FC Barcelona. Fans of all ages will enjoy the **Museo Real Madrid** that charts the club's history and includes a tour of the stadium. Museum and tour tickets are sold from Window 10, near Gate 7, on the Paseo de la Castellana (☎ **91-398-43-70, 90-230-17-09;** www.realmadrid.es). Admission costs 15€ for adults, 10€ for under-14s. Hours are Monday to Saturday 10:30am to 7:30pm, Sunday and public holidays 10:30am to 6:30pm. There's limited access on match days.

7 ★★ kids **Museo del Traje.** Madrid's costume museum opened in 2004, and has become—fittingly—quite fashionable. The permanent collection (which rotates regularly) contains everything from the heartbreakingly tiny medieval burial gown of the Infanta María to the jaunty costumes of the Madrileño *majos* and *majas*

Museo del Traje.

(working-class dandies) depicted by Goya. Fashionistas will love the delicate designer pieces from the 20th century, ranging from embroidered flapper dresses to chic eveningwear by the legendary Balenciaga. Fashion-conscious teenagers will love this place, but children of all ages will enjoy trying on the old-fashioned outfits, as well as strutting down the catwalk at the exit. ⏰ *45 min. Av. Juan de Herrera 2.* ☎ *91-550-47-00. http://museodeltraje.mcu.es. Adults 3€, 1.50€ students, free 17 and under and 65 and over. Tues–Sat 9:30am–7pm, Sun and public hols 10am–3pm; open until 10:30pm on Thurs in July and Aug. Closed Mon. Metro: Moncloa.*

8 ★★ **Bokado.** This chic restaurant (p 102) in the Museo del Traje has an adjoining cafe, with a pleasant summer terrace overlooking the fountains and velvety lawns. On a hot summer evening, it's blissful. *Museo del Traje 9.* ☎ *91-549-00-41. www.bokadogrupo.com. Main dishes 17€–30€, tapas (in cafe) 3€–9€.*

Madrid for Kids

1. Museo del Ferrocarril
2. Dining Car
3. Boating in the Parque del Retiro
4. Museo Real Madrid
5. Babydeli
6. Museo de Ciencias Naturales
7. Teleférico
8. Parque de Atracciones
9. Zoo
10. Home Burger

- (i) Information
- 🏛 Museum
- 🚉 Train Station
- Ⓜ Metro

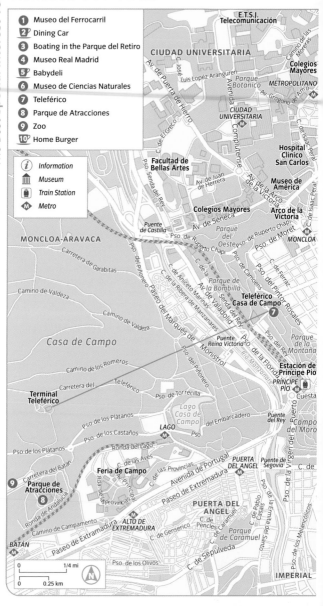

Madrid's art museums may leave your children cold, but the city has plenty to offer younger visitors. They can mess about on boats, ride a steam train, float across the city in a cable car, roar at the lions in the zoo, or just kick a ball around one of the glorious parks. At the end of a long day, Madrid's tapas bars provide child-sized portions and open earlier than restaurants. START: **Metro to Delicias.**

① ★★ Museo del Ferrocarril. The hugely enjoyable train museum has a collection of historic trains for kids to clamber over and pretend to drive, plus model railways to race, and a beautifully restored 1920s' dining car. It offers discounted admission on Saturday mornings. ⏱ 1 hr. Paseo de las Delicias 61. ☎ 90-222-88-22. www.museodel ferrocarril.org. Adults 5€, 3.50€ children 4–12, 1€ on Sat; free for under-4s. Tues–Sun 10am–3pm; closed Mon. Metro: Delicias.

②★ Dining Car. I love this beautifully restored dining car, with its plush wood paneling and flip-up leather seats. It's good for coffee and chocolate milk, but doesn't have much in the way of snacks. Museo del Ferrocarril. ☎ 90-222-88-22. Coffee 2€.

③ ★★ Boating in the Parque del Retiro. The Retiro Gardens are heaven for kids of all ages. There are several play areas (including an adventure playground) near the Puerta de Alcalá entrance, but best of all is the boating lake. Bring bread to feed the koi or take out a rowing boat. If you'd rather let someone (or something) else do the work, take a trip on a little solar-powered boat. ⏱ 1 hr. No phone. Parque del Retiro. Rowing boats available 10am–dusk, 4.50€; solar-powered boat trip 1.15€, free under-2s, runs 10am–dusk. Metro: Retiro or Banco de España.

Boating lake in Parque del Retiro.

④ ★★ Museo Real Madrid. ⏱ 1 hr. See p 47.

⑤★ Babydeli. This organic deli-cum-cafe, set up by three mums, has a garden play area, delicious snacks, and fun workshops for children aged 0 to 8. C/ Lagasca 54. ☎ 91-576-38-10. www.babydeli. com. Snacks 4€–10€.

⑥ ★★ Museo de Ciencias Naturales. The cabinets of stuffed animals—especially the gigantic squid—and huge dinosaur skeletons will keep kids enthralled. ⏱ 1 hr. C/ Joé Gutierrez Abascal 2. ☎ 91-411-13-28. www.mncn.csic.es. Adults 5€; 3€ children 4–14 and students; free children 3 and under and adults 65 and over. Tues–Fri

Kids' Attractions Around Madrid

There are plenty of big theme parks around Madrid to keep children happy for at least a day. Hang out with Daffy Duck and Yogi Bear at the **Parque Warner,** San Martín de la Vega (☎ 91-808-76-00; www.parquewarner.com; 39€ adults, 30€ kids under 140cm (1.4 m); local train to Parque del Ocio or bus to Vaillaverde, then shuttle bus); enjoy the penguins and flamingoes at the botanic park, **Faunia,** Av. de las Comunidades (☎ 91-301-62-10; www.faunia.es; 25.50€ adults, 19.50€ children 3–8, free under 3s; Metro to Valdebernardo, local train to Vicalvaro, bus 71 to Plaza Manuel Becerra); or beat the summer heat at the **Aquopolis** water park (www.aquopolis.es). Children can even learn to ski at an indoor ski-center, in Xanadú Shopping Center (☎ 90-236-13-09; www.madridsnowzone.com; entry plus equipment hire for 1hr. 18€; bus 528, 534, or 539 from Príncipe Pío), open year-round.

10am–6pm, Sat 10am–8pm (closes at 3pm July–Aug), Sun 10am–2:30pm. Closed Mon, Jan 1, May 1, Dec 25. Metro: Gregario Marañón.

7 ★★ **Teleférico.** ⏱ 30 min. See p 87, **1**.

8 ★ **Parque de Atracciones.** For thrill-seekers, there's nowhere better than Madrid's Attraction Park in the Casa de Campo. Older kids

Thrills in the Parque de Atracciones.

will love the Abismo rollercoaster or the head-spinning Rotor, while smaller children can enjoy a host of gentler rides. ⏱ 2 hr. See p 51, **8**.

9 ★ **Zoo.** A short walk beyond the Parque de Atracciones is Madrid's zoo-aquarium. Pandas, elephants, tigers, dolphins, and a petting zoo will keep your children happily entertained. ⏱ 2 hr. ☎ 91-512-37-70. www.zoomadrid.com. Adults 19.40€, 15.70€ children 3–7 and seniors, free 2 and under. Opening hours vary from week to week, but are approximately daily 11am–6pm in winter, 10:30am–7pm in summer, later at weekends. Check the website or inquire via the tourist office. Closed Jan. Metro: Casa de Campo, or cable car and a 15-min walk.

10 ★ **Home Burger.** Decked out in retro '60s' style, this serves the best burgers in town—all organic, with a range of options. Great veggie burgers, too. C/ Silva 25. ☎ 91-115-12-79. www.homeburgerbar.com. Burgers 9.75€–12€.

Tapas Tour of Madrid

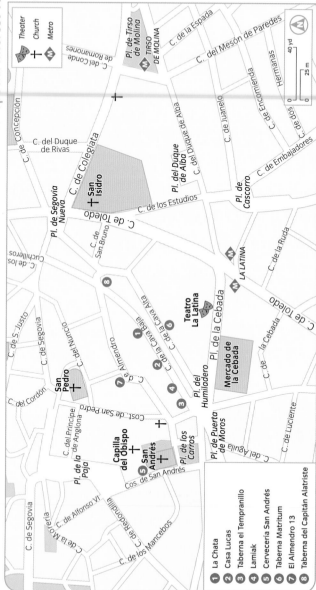

Theater
Church
Metro

1 La Chata
2 Casa Lucas
3 Taberna el Tempranillo
4 Lamiak
5 Cervecería San Andrés
6 Taberna Matritum
7 El Almendro 13
8 Taberna del Capitán Alatriste

Tapas are central to Madrid's culinary scene, and a tour of the city's tapas bars is one of the most convivial and enjoyable gourmet experiences anywhere. I've chosen one of the most popular bar districts in the city, La Latina, which is always jam-packed after the Rastro market. Visit during the week to avoid the crowds.
START: **Metro to La Latina. Trip length: half-day or evening.**

1 ★ La Chata. Cava Baja descends from the Plaza Segovia, and is jam-packed with popular tapas bars. La Chata is colorfully tiled and filled with hanging hams. The house specialty is *rabo de toro* (stewed bull's tail), but I also recommend the Andaluz-style fried fish (*fritura de pescado*). 🕐 *30 min. C/ Cava Baja 24.* ☎ *91-366-14-58. Closed Tues and Wed lunchtimes. Metro: La Latina.*

2 ★★★ Casa Lucas. Farther down on the right, tiny Casa Lucas has an excellent selection of wines by the glass and the tapas are fresh and creative. 🕐 *30 min. C/ Cava Baja 30.* ☎ *91-365-08-04. www. casalucas.es. Closed Wed lunchtime. Metro: La Latina.*

3 ★★ Taberna el Tempranillo. A favorite with locals, this low-key bar has particularly good wines and some original tapas. The hams, which include a selection of unusual cuts, are always a tempting option. 🕐 *30 min. C/ Cava Baja 30.* ☎ *91-364-15-32. Metro: La Latina.*

4 ★★ Lamiak. This modern bar specializes in Basque *pintxos*—slices of crusty baguette with any imaginable topping. Try them with a glass of refreshing *Txacoli* (a young Basque white wine). 🕐 *30 min. C/ Cava Baja 42.* ☎ *91-365-52-12. www.lamiak.net. Closed Sun eve and all day Mon. Metro: La Latina.*

5 ★ Cervecería San Andrés. Cava Baja emerges into the Plaza del Humilladero and almost opposite is the Cervecería San Andrés, with a large summer terrace. Cool off with an ice-cold *caña* and fill up on classic tapas such as *patatas bravas*. 🕐 *30 min. Plaza de San Andrés 4.* ☎ *91-366-55-51. Metro: La Latina.*

The colorful facade of La Chata.

Tapas for Beginners

Tapas in Madrid range from simple dishes of olives to gourmet creations prepared with foams and foie gras. But most traditional bars in the city serve the following classics. *Croquetas*, mashed-potato croquettes, come with various fillings, usually *jamón* (ham) or *bacalao* (cod). *Patatas bravas*, chunks of fried potato smothered in a spicy sauce, are said to have been invented here. *Tortilla*, a thick potato omelet, is another classic. Many places serve shellfish, conserved in oil and vinegar: Try *mejillones* (mussels), *almejas* (clams), or *anchoas* (anchovies). These are all commonly accompanied with a glass of draught beer (*una caña*) or wine (*vino tinto* is red, *vino blanco* is white, *vino rosado* is rosé).

⑥ ★★★ Taberna Matritum. Parallel to Cava Baja is another bar-lined street, the Cava Alta. On the right is the Taberna Matritum, intimate and elegant, which specializes in wines, including boutique labels and rare vintages. Ask the helpful staff for advice. Among my favorite tapas are the eggplants (aubergines) baked with sun-dried tomatoes, and they also have delicious desserts. If you have the strength, you can continue up Cava Alta to find numerous excellent tapas bars,

Taberna Matritum.

including **Cava Blanca** at no. 7 (☎ 91-365-05-03). ⏱ *30 min. C/ Cava Alta 16.* ☎ *91-365-82-37. www.matritum.es. Evenings only except weekends. Metro: La Latina.*

⑦ ★ El Almendro 13. Yet more bars can be found along crooked Calle Almendro, which also runs roughly parallel to Cava Baja. This unassuming but authentic tavern is great for an ice-cold *fino* (sherry) on a hot summer's day, or a heaped plate of fried eggs and ham in winter. ⏱ *30 min. C/ Alemendro 13.* ☎ *91-365-42-52. Metro: La Latina.*

⑧ ★★★ Taberna del Capitán Alatriste. This traditional inn, with its wooden beams and brick-lined cellar, emulates the 16th-century taverns where novelist Pérez-Reverte's swashbuckling hero, Captain Alatriste, would have arranged assignations. Try the partridge pie, prepared to a medieval recipe. ⏱ *30 min. C/ Grafal 7.* ☎ *91-366-18-83. www.tabernadel capitanalatriste.com. Closed Mon. Metro: La Latina.* ●

The Best Neighborhood Walks

Santa Ana: **Barrio de las Letras**

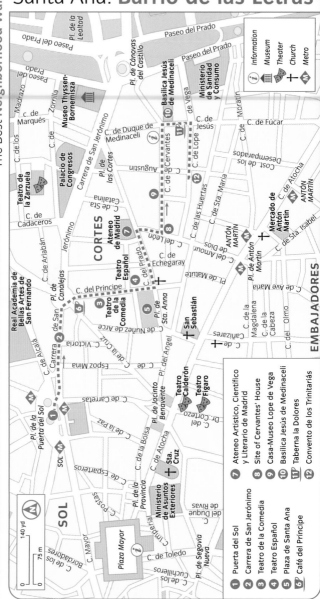

Information
Museum
Theater
Church
Metro

1 Puerta del Sol
2 Carrera de San Jerónimo
3 Teatro de la Comedia
4 Teatro Español
5 Plaza de Santa Ana
6 Café del Príncipe
7 Ateneo Artístico, Científico y Literario de Madrid
8 Site of Cervantes' House
9 Casa-Museo Lope de Vega
10 Basílica Jesús de Medinaceli
11 Taberna la Dolores
12 Convento de los Trinitarías

Previous page: Plaza de España:

S anta Ana has long been the most bohemian *barrio* in Madrid. Writers and dramatists such as Cervantes and Lope de Vega lived (and bickered) here during the Golden Age of the 16th century, and intellectuals argued about poetry and politics in the legendary 19th-century cafes and bars. Memories of literary giants live on in the historic streets. START: **Metro to Sol.** **Trip length: half-day.**

1 ★ Puerta del Sol. 🕐 *20 min.* See p 7, **2**.

2 ★ Carrera de San Jerónimo.
Walk down the Carrera de San Jerónimo, pausing at the **Fontana del Oro,** now an Irish pub, but formerly a celebrated 19th-century literary cafe where Benito Pérez Galdós, one of the most important Spanish novelists of the 20th century, penned his first novel. At no. 8 is **L'Hardy,** a magnificently unchanged restaurant that has been a favorite with writers since it opened in 1839. Queen Isabella II is said to have entertained her lovers in the upstairs dining room. 🕐 *20 min.*

3 ★ Teatro de la Comedia.
When King Alfonso XII in 1875 inaugurated the Teatro de la Comedia, with its wrought-iron twirls, at Calle del Príncipe 14, it was considered the most modern, beautiful, and comfortable theater in the city. Now

Teatro de la Comedia.

the seat of the **Compañía Nacional de Teatro Clásico,** which stages excellent Spanish classical drama, it

Cervantes & *Don Quijote*

Don Quijote is possibly the most famous literary character in the world. The tale of the deluded knight, who with the help of his portly sidekick Sancho Panza tilted at windmills and sought the love of Dulcinea, is a much-loved classic. Miguel de Cervantes (1547–1616), the author of *Don Quijote,* led almost as exciting a life as his gangling knight, participating in great sea battles, being captured and enslaved, and returning to Spain only to spend years in debtors' prison. International recognition (although little financial reward) came with the publication of *Don Quijote* in 1605, but Cervantes was broke once again when he died in 1616.

is currently closed for refurbishment. (The theater company is temporarily based at the Teatro Pavón.) 🕐 *10 min.*

④ ★★ Teatro Español. The Teatro Español is the city's most historic theater, and has its origins in a 16th-century corral, although the current building dates back only to 1807. Many great Spanish masterpieces have had their premiers here, including Lorca's *Yerma*, which opened in 1934 (and was received with jeers and rotten fruit). 🕐 *10 min. C/ Príncipe 35.* ☎ *91-360-14-84. Metro: Sol.*

⑤ ★★ kids Plaza de Santa Ana. The heart of the Barrio de las Letras neighborhood, this huge square is lined with bars and cafes. Kids squeal in the playgrounds as their parents watch from the terrace cafes, and itinerant musicians make

The Teatro Español is the city's most historic theater.

their beady-eyed way from tourist to tourist. 🕐 *30 min. Metro: Sol.*

⑥ Café del Príncipe. This sumptuous, wood-paneled cafe preserves its original 19th-century decor and is perfect for breakfast or a coffee break. *Plaza de Canalejas 5.* ☎ *91-531-81-83. Coffee and a pastry 2.50€.*

⑦ Ateneo Artístico, Científico y Literario de Madrid. This venerable institution was founded in 1820 and established here since the 1930s to promote the study of the arts and sciences. The gloriously old-fashioned library (closed to the public), with its glossy wooden stacks, remains a magnificent testament to Enlightenment-era ideals. 🕐 *10 min. C/ Prado 21. Metro: Antón Martín.*

⑧ Site of Cervantes' House. Very few places associated with poor Cervantes, universally recognized as Spain's greatest writer, have survived the centuries. His modest home, which once stood here on a long-gone square, was demolished in 1833, and a marble plaque is all that remains. 🕐 *10 min. C/ León (at corner of C/ Cervantes).*

⑨ ★★ Casa-Museo Lope de Vega. Lope de Vega (1562–1635) was a prolific dramatist, creating some of the greatest plays of the 16th century. Here, in his charmingly restored home, he took refuge from his chaotic love life (two wives, several mistresses, and a spell in prison after being spurned by a pretty Madrileña called Elena Osirio), and churned out an immense body of work in his study. Visits by guided tour only: Book in advance. 🕐 *30 min. C/ Cervantes 11.* ☎ *91-429-92-16. Tues–Sun 10am–3pm. Closed Mon. Metro: Antón Martín.*

⑩ ★ **Basílica Jesús de Medinaceli.** This church, completed in 1930, is dedicated to the protection of one of the most venerated statues in the city, the 17th-century *Cristo de Medinaceli*. According to legend, the statue was stolen by North African armies, who demanded a ransom equaling its weight in gold. However, when the statue was placed on the scales, it was found, miraculously, to weigh only as much as a single coin.

⑪ ★ **Taberna la Dolores.** Lavishly tiled and resolutely old-fashioned, this popular tapas bar is a beacon of continuity in a *barrio* ruffled by change and gentrification. *Plaza de Jesús 4.* ☎ *91-429-22-43. Beer and montadito 3.50€.*

⑫ ★ **Convento de los Trinitariás.** Both Cervantes and Lope de Vega had daughters who became nuns behind the forbidding brick

Plaque commemorating Lope de Vega.

During the Golden Age, the three most beautiful actresses (all named María) would attend Sunday mass in their finery, to the distraction of the congregation and the fury of the priest. A crowd of hundreds gathers on Friday evenings to kiss the feet of the statue. 🕐 *15 min. C/ del Duque de Medinaceli s/n.* ☎ *91-364-40-50. Daily 8am–12:30pm and 6–9pm. Metro: Antón Martín.*

wall of the Convento de los Trinitariás, and when Cervantes died, poverty-stricken, in 1516, he was buried in the convent church. Unfortunately, his bones (like those of Lope de Vega) were lost, and his life is commemorated only by a large marble plaque on the wall. 🕐 *15 min. C/ Lope de Vega s/n. Metro: Antón Martín.*

Chueca & Malasaña: Shopping & Nightlife

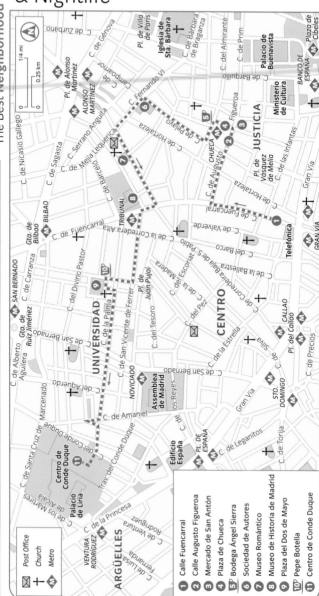

1 Calle Fuencarral
2 Calle Augusto Figueroa
3 Mercado de San Antón
4 Plaza de Chueca
5 Bodega Ángel Sierra
6 Sociedad de Autores
7 Museo Romántico
8 Plaza del Dos de Mayo
9 Museo de Historia de Madrid
10 Pepe Botella
11 Centro de Conde Duque

The boho-chic areas of Chueca and Malasaña have boomed recently, although they remain appealingly scruffy around the edges. Chueca, the vibrant gay district, boasts designer boutiques and restaurants, while Malasaña's bars attract a young, alternative crowd. In the middle, the triBall district injects new life with bars and offbeat shops. START: **Metro to Gran Vía. Trip length: half-day.**

Shoe shopping on Calle Augusto Figueroa.

① ★ **Calle Fuencarral.** This semi-pedestrianized street has been utterly transformed in the last few years. Once known for junkies and prostitution, it's now lined with trees and international fashion boutiques (my favorites include Barcelona label **Custo** at no. 29 and the Basque firm **Hoss Intropia** at no. 16). The street marks the eastern boundary of the offbeat but über-stylish triBall district (see below). ⏱ *20 min. Metro: Gran Vía.*

② ★ **Calle Augusto Figueroa.** I love shoes and several designer outlet stores are clustered here, with a wide range of gorgeous footwear for men and women. Rummage for designs by Pura López, Farrutx (which has a dedicated outlet at no. 18), Dorotea, and Audley. ⏱ *30 min. Metro: Chueca.*

③ ★ **Mercado de San Antón.** The neighborhood's shiny new market has produce stalls selling fish, meat, and vegetables on the ground floor, plus a host of Spanish and international deli items (to eat in or take away) upstairs. It's topped off with a rooftop restaurant that has a terrace. ⏱ *20 min. Metro: Chueca.*

④ ★ **Plaza de Chueca.** Calle Barbieri (opposite the Mercado) whisks you to the heart of the neighborhood, the delightful Plaza de Chueca. Old-fashioned '60s-style cafes rub up against chic boutiques such as **L'Habilleur** at no. 8 (☎ 91-531-32-22) with designer bargains, all presided over by the historic, wood-paneled **Bodega Ángel Sierra.** ⏱ *30 min. Metro: Chueca.*

triBall: Madrid's SoHo

The city's latest "hot" neighborhood is triBall, enclosed by Gran Vía, Calle Fuencarral, and Corredera Baja de San Pablo. A haunt popular with supermodels, actors, and fashionistas, this once-grotty district is now replete with alternative boutiques, galleries, workshops, restaurants, and bars. Among my favorite spots are the bordello-turned-boutique **La Maison de la Lanterne Rouge,** Calle Ballesta 4 (☎ 91-310-79-61; http://lalinternaroja.blogspot.com/), which boasts a stunning mural by Santiago Morilla and has a great mix of fashion, interior decoration, and art. For lunch, try the '50s-style **Lunch Box & Tiki,** Calle Barco 8 (☎ 91-523-33-64), which sells gourmet sandwiches for around 8€. For a full directory, see www.triballmadrid.com.

5 ★★ Bodega Ángel Sierra.
One of Madrid's oldest surviving taverns, this exquisite bodega is an obligatory stopping point in Chueca. I was brought here on one of my very first visits to the city, and introduced to the perfect pairing of chilled *vermut* (vermouth) with an anchovy wrapped around an olive. *Plaza Chueca 11.* ☎ *91-531-01-26. Vermut and olives 3.50€.*

6 ★★ Sociedad de Autores.
Decorated with icing-sugar swirls, the creamy **Palacio Longoria**

Sociedad de Autores.

(1902) is the finest *Modernista* building in Madrid, and is currently home to the Society of Authors, which gathers royalties for Spanish writers. The palace is not open to the public, but you could try sweet-talking the doorman to let you look at the sweeping staircase. ⏱ *15 min. C/ Fernando VI 4.* ☎ *91-349-95-50. Metro: Alonso Martínez.*

7 ★★ Museo Romántico.
The Marqués de Vega-Inclán (1858–1942) was a magpie collector, whose varied collection of paintings, musical instruments, folk costumes, and curiosities are now gathered in a graceful 18th-century townhouse. The salons have been prettily furnished to evoke the atmosphere of a wealthy middle-class Madrileño home in the mid-19th century. There's a charming cafe for refreshments, complete with patio garden. ⏱ *45 min. C/ San Mateo 13.* ☎ *91-448-10-65. http:// en.museoromanticismo.mcu.es. May–Oct Mon–Sat 9:30am–8:30pm, Sun 10am–3pm; Nov–Apr Mon–Sat 9:30am–6:30pm, Sun 10am–3pm. Adults 3€, free children 17 and under and adults 65 and over. Free Sat from 2pm. Metro: Tribunal.*

8 ★ Museo de Historia de Madrid. The 18th-century Hospital of San Fernando, now the city history museum, boasts a fabulous Churrigueresque doorway, encrusted with extravagant swirls, by baroque architect Pedro de Ribera. The museum is currently undergoing a massive restoration and was closed at the time of writing. ⏱ *10 min. C/ Fuencarral 78.* ☎ *91-701-18-63. www.esmadrid. com/museodehistoria. Metro: Tribunal.*

9 ★★ kids Plaza del Dos de Mayo. This is one of my favorite Madrileño squares. During the day, the split-level square is quiet—apart from the children in the little playground. By night, it's packed with young people, who fill the bars and the square. The name commemorates a tragic event in Madrid's history, the massacre of citizens by Napoleon's troops, which took place on May 2, 1808. (Goya commemorated the event in his famous painting, *Dos de Mayo*, which hangs in the Prado.) A local seamstress, Manuel Malasaña, now a folk hero, was shot for defending herself with her scissors. The two army commanders, Daoíz and Velarde, who organized the unsuccessful revolt against the French occupiers, are commemorated in a double statue.

The archway behind them is all that remains of their barracks, which formerly occupied the square. ⏱ *10 min.*

10 Pepe Botella. A classic on the corner of the Plaza del Dos de Mayo, this shabby-chic cafe-bar is a big favorite with an alternative, arty crowd of actors, film directors, and writers. It's a mellow spot for a coffee during the day, but gets lively at night. *C/ San Andrés 12.* ☎ *91-522-43-09. Beer 2€.*

11 ★★ Centro de Conde Duque. The streets around the Plaza del Dos de Mayo, especially Calle San Vicente Ferrer, Calle Pez, and Calle Espiritu Santo, are crammed with bars. There are even more around the Conde Duque arts center. This immense red-brick edifice with a lavish baroque portal was built in 1717 to house the Royal Guards. Now it's an important cultural institution, with a wide-ranging program of art exhibitions, concerts, and festivals. Closed at press time for extensive refurbishment, it's slated to reopen in 2013. ⏱ *1 hr. C/ Conde Duque 11.* ☎ *91-588-58-34. www.esmadrid.com/ condeduque. Metro: Ventura Rodriguez.*

Plaza del Dos de Mayo.

La Latina & Lavapiés

1 Taberna Tirso de Molina
2 Plaza de Tirso de Molina
3 Colegiata de San Isidro
4 Mercado de la Cebada
5 Capilla de San Isidro
6 Museo de los Orígenes (Casa San Isidro)
7 La Taberna Errante
8 Basílica de San Francisco el Grande
9 Iglesia Virgen de la Paloma
10 El Rastro (Calle de la Ribera de Curtidores)
11 La Corrala
12 Plaza de Lavapiés

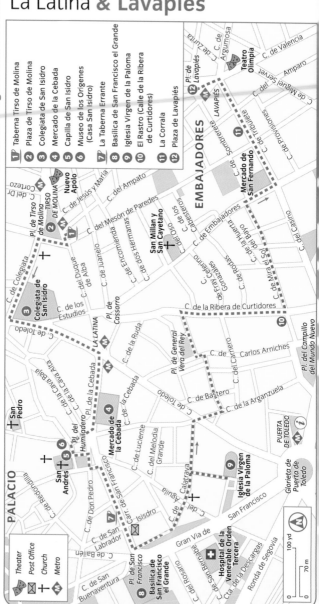

Legend:
🎭 Theater
✉ Post Office
✝ Church
◆ Metro

The ramshackle neighborhoods of La Latina and Lavapiés sprawl downhill from the Plaza Mayor. Traditionally occupied by the city's poor, the areas are today multicultural and increasingly gentrified. This tour is best on Sunday, when you can enjoy the Rastro flea market and follow it with a tapas tour of La Latina's stylish bars. START: **Metro to Tirso de Molina. Trip length: half-day.**

1 ★ **Taberna Tirso de Molina.** Start with breakfast or some tapas at this pretty Art Nouveau-style cafe. *Plaza de Tirso de Molina 9.* ☎ *91-429-17-56. Coffee and a pastry 2.50€.*

2 ★ **kids Plaza de Tirso de Molina.** Local children play in the playground as their parents watch from the terrace cafes, and flower-sellers operate from modern wood-and-steel cabins. It's named after the Golden Age dramatist Tirso de Molina (1583–1648), whose statue overlooks the square. ⏱ *20 min. Metro: Tirso de Molina.*

3 ★★ **Colegiata de San Isidro.** This massive baroque church was built by the Jesuits in the 17th century but, after they were expelled from Spain in 1767, it was revamped and rededicated to the city's beloved patron saint, San Isidro, and his wife. Their remains are displayed in elaborate urns in the main altar. ⏱ *20 min. C/ Toledo 37.* ☎ *91-364-40-50. Open for mass only. Metro: La Latina.*

4 ★ **Mercado de la Cebada.** The '60s-style exterior may not appeal to all, but inside you'll find a wonderful range of top-quality fruit, vegetables, meat, and fresh fish (except Mon). ⏱ *40 min. Plaza de la Cebada s/n.* ☎ *91-365-91-76. Mon–Sat 8:30am–2:30pm and 5:30–8:30pm. Metro: La Latina.*

5 ★ **Capilla de San Isidro.** A sumptuous baroque confection topped with a dome, this was built

Mercado de la Cebada.

El Rastro, Calle Ribera de Curtidores.

in the late 17th century to contain the remains of Madrid's revered patron saint, San Isidro. (They were later transferred to the Colegiata de San Isidro, **❸**.) ⏲ *30 min. Plaza de San Andrés 1.* ☎ *91-365-48-71. Mon–Thurs and Sat 8am–1pm and 6–8pm. Free admission. Metro: La Latina.*

❻ ★ Museo de los Orígenes (Casa San Isidro). The Museum of Origins is housed in an old palace that preserves the very well from which San Isidro is said to have plucked his drowned son and restored him to life (see box, below). The museum offers an interesting glimpse into Madrid's early history, with plans, photographs, and archaeological finds ⏲ *30 min. Plaza de San Andrés 2.* ☎ *91-366-74-15. Sept–July Tues–Fri 9:30am–8pm, Sat–Sun 10am–2pm; Aug Tues–Fri 9:30am–2:30pm, Sat–Sun 10am–2pm. Closed Mon. Free admission. Metro: La Latina.*

❼ ★ La Taberna Errante. This friendly inn serves delicious market-fresh food. Try the mussels, prepared by a charming singing chef. *C/ San Francisco, 8.* ☎ *91-530-94-42. Closed Mon. Main dishes 7€–12€.*

❽ ★★ Basílica de San Francisco el Grande. Despite royal protection and even a short-lived stint as pantheon for great Spaniards, the vast neoclassical Basílica is now best known for its lavish decoration and an early painting by Goya, St. Bernardino of Siena Preaching to Alfonso V of Aragon (1781–83), in a side chapel. A small (and frankly dull) museum contains a collection of religious art: The dahlia gardens next to it are much nicer. ⏲ *30 min. Plaza de San Francisco 11.* ☎ *91-365-38-00. Tues–Sat 10am–1pm and 4–6:30pm. Adults 3€. Metro: La Latina.*

⑨ ★ Iglesia Virgen de la Paloma. This is the spiritual heart of La Latina and home to a venerated 18th-century painting of the Virgin. The annual festival held in her honor (Aug 15) is a touching affair, with a solemn parade followed by a huge street party. ⏱ *30 min. Plaza Virgen de la Paloma.* ☎ *91-365-46-69. www.archimadrid. es/lapaloma. Tues–Sat 11:15am– 12:45pm and 5:15–7pm. Adults 3€. Metro: La Latina.*

⑩ ★★★ El Rastro (Calle Ribera de Curtidores). Beyond Calle Mira del Rio Alta, which is lined with bric-a-brac stores full of unexpected treasures, is Madrid's celebrated flea market, El Rastro, which dates back to the Middle Ages. It takes place on the steep Calle Ribera de Curtidores every Sunday morning, attracting a huge crowd of locals, tourists—and those who prey on them. Keep a very close eye on your belongings. It's a colorful spectacle, with stalls selling everything from car parts to antiques, African crafts to Asian jewelry. ⏱ *1 hr. C/ Ribera de Curtidores and surrounding streets. Market held Sun mornings. Metro: Puerta de Toledo or La Latina.*

⑪ La Corrala. A century or so ago, these neighborhoods were filled with *corralas*, humble timber-framed apartment blocks set around a courtyard. Few have survived, but this one was renovated in the late 1970s and still occasionally provides an unusual setting for flamenco concerts or other events (the tourist office can provide information). ⏱ *10 min. C/ del Mesón de Paredes, between C/ Tribulete and C/ Sombrerete. Metro: Lavapiés.*

⑫ ★ Plaza de Lavapiés. Once the heart of the Jewish ghetto, before the expulsion of the Jews from Spain in 1492, the Plaza de Lavapiés is now the center of Madrid's most multi-cultural *barrio*. Just as in the past, when these *barrios bajos* ("low neighborhoods") were home to immigrants from the rest of Spain, hoping to find work and a chance for a better life, so now they are home to immigrants from farther afield. In fact, it's estimated that about 50% of the residents of Lavapiés were born outside Spain. ⏱ *15 min. Metro: Lavapiés.*

San Isidro: Madrid's Patron Saint

Madrid's biggest traditional festival is held on May 15 in honor of the city's patron saint, San Isidro. A humble laborer in 11th-century Madrid, Isidro was credited with numerous miracles, including raising several people—not least his young son—from the dead. His feast day is celebrated with a solemn mass at the Colegiata de San Isidro, processions, and popular street parties. Isidro's wife María was also a saint, and is almost as revered by Madrileños. Their remains sit together on the high altar at the Colegiata de San Isidro.

The Best Neighborhood Walks

Traditional **Madrid**

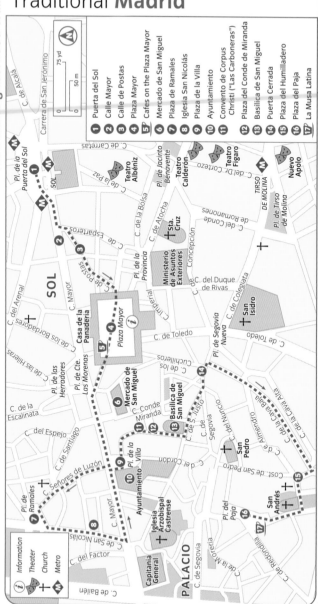

- ① Puerta del Sol
- ② Calle Mayor
- ③ Calle de Postas
- ④ Plaza Mayor
- ⑤ Cafes on the Plaza Mayor
- ⑥ Mercado de San Miguel
- ⑦ Plaza de Ramales
- ⑧ Iglesia San Nicolás
- ⑨ Plaza de la Villa
- ⑩ Ayuntamiento
- ⑪ Convento de Corpus Christi ("Las Carboneras")
- ⑫ Plaza del Conde de Miranda
- ⑬ Basílica de San Miguel
- ⑭ Puerta Cerrada
- ⑮ Plaza del Humilladero
- ⑯ Plaza de la Paja
- ⑰ La Musa Latina

Information ℹ
Theater ◸
Church ✝
Metro ◈

The old heart of Madrid is an atmospheric maze of narrow streets, secret squares, and beautiful churches. This tour meanders through the ancient core, taking in well-known monuments and lingering in secluded corners. This is a good walk for foodies, with gourmet treats in the Mercado de San Miguel and handmade candy passed through a convent gate. START: **Metro to Sol. Trip length: half-day.**

1 ★★ Puerta del Sol. During the 16th century, visitors to the newly established Spanish capital gathered at one of three meeting places to find work, exchange gossip, visit the markets, and prey on new arrivals. Our visit begins at the first of these, the Puerta del Sol (we'll visit the other two— the Plaza Mayor and the Plaza de la Villa—later). ⏱ *20 min. See p 7, 2.*

2 ★ Calle Mayor. This was, as its name suggests, the main street of the old city, linking the Puerta del Sol with the Plaza Mayor. Although long eclipsed by modern avenues such as the Gran Vía, it's still full of life, with a string of busy shops and bars. ⏱ *20 min. Metro: Sol.*

Attractive street sign on Calle Mayor.

3 Calle de Postas. Plunge into old Madrid via the ancient Calle de Postas. Despite the souvenir shops and tourists, this attractive, semi-pedestrianized street manages to retain a strong flavor of the past. It's named after the first post office, which stood here until it was moved to the Puerta del Sol in the 18th century. **The Posada del Peine,** now a boutique hotel, has occupied the same building at no. 17 for almost 4 centuries, making it one of the oldest inns in town. ⏱ *20 min. Metro: Sol.*

4 ★★★ kids Plaza Mayor. The immense Plaza Mayor is completely enclosed by handsome baroque buildings, with access to the central square provided by several archways. ⏱ *40 min. See p 7, 1.*

CALLE MAYOR

Plaza Mayor.

5 Cafes on the Plaza Mayor.
Take your pick of several cafes on the Plaza Mayor, most of which boast great terraces. If you want to blend in with the locals, pick one in the shade. Or join the pink-faced northern European tourists and soak up the sun. Stick with coffee or drinks—for lunch, you'll do much better elsewhere. **Coffee from 2.50€.**

6 Mercado de San Miguel.
This elegant, airy, glass-and-steel market was erected between 1913 and 1916, and has recently been transformed into a gastronomic hot spot. The stalls specialize in the finest produce, from hams to olive oil, and from exotic imports to fine wines. It's a great place to stop for a mid-morning pick-me-up. ⏱ *30 min. Plaza de San Miguel s/n. www.mercadodesanmiguel.es. Mon–Wed and Sun 10am–midnight; Thurs–Sat 10am–2am. Metro: Sol.*

7 ★★ Plaza de Ramales.
An elegant square fringed with terrace cafes, the Plaza de Ramales was originally named after the Iglesia de San Juan, where the great Spanish painter Velázquez was buried in 1660. His bones were lost when Joseph Bonaparte ordered the destruction of the church in 1808. ⏱ *10 min. Plaza de Ramales. Metro: Ópera.*

8 ★★ Iglesia de San Nicolás.
The city's oldest church, the Iglesia de San Nicolás was built over the ruins of a former mosque in the 12th century. The pretty brick minaret was preserved to form a steeple. *Plaza de San Nicolás 48. ☎ 91-369-05-79. Open for mass only. Metro: Ópera.*

The Plaza de la Villa contains an ensemble of fine buildings.

Take a tour to view the City Hall's impressive baroque ceilings.

9 ★★★ **Plaza de la Villa.** An enchanting square, this boasts a superb ensemble of ancient buildings. On the left is the **Torre de los Lujanes,** with its sturdy square tower and cream stripes. This is the oldest palace in the city, built during the 15th century. Here, so legend has it, Francis I of France was kept prisoner until a ransom was raised. Opposite is the handsome **Casa de la Villa** (formerly the City Hall, see **10**). The third building is the **Casa de Cisneros,** a graceful 16th-century palace with Plateresque decoration—and the palace I'd buy if I were a millionaire. ⏱ *30 min. Plaza de la Villa. Metro: Ópera or Sol.*

10 ★★ **Ayuntamiento.** The Casa de la Villa (City Hall) was completed at the end of the 17th century and endowed with some flamboyant baroque flourishes. Unfortunately, very little of the original interior has survived, and the tours (book at the tourist office) are uniformly dull. Three rooms break the monotony: The **Salón de Recepciones,** with an exquisitely painted baroque ceiling; the original **patio,** now covered with a stained-glass ceiling; and the 19th-century velvet-and-gilt **Salón de Plenos.** ⏱ *1 hr. Plaza de la Villa. Book tours, which take place Mon at 5pm, through the tourist office (p 160), Tours in English and Spanish. Free admission. Metro: Ópera or Sol.*

11 ★ **Convento de Corpus Christi ("Las Carboneras").** This convent tucked around the corner from the Plaza de la Villa, through the narrow passage next to the Torre de los Lujanes, is a wonderful time-capsule. You can enter the silent church for a moment's contemplation, or pick up some of the nuns' sweet treats by ringing the doorbell. By ancient tradition, the candy is delivered through a revolving drawer into which you put your money. ⏱ *20 min. Plaza del Conde de Miranda 3.* ☎ *93-476-57-21. Sweets sold 9:30am–1pm and 4–6:30pm. Metro: Ópera.*

12 **Plaza del Conde de Miranda.** This charming little square is one of the oldest in the city, still flanked by fine mansions

The Best Neighborhood Walks

Capilla del Obispo in the Plaza del Paja.

including the sumptuous residence built for the 18th-century Conde de Miranda. There's an art market on summer weekends. ⏲ *10 min. Plaza del Conde de Miranda 3. Metro: Ópera.*

⑬ Basílica de San Miguel. This impressive 18th-century basilica is now administered by the Opus Dei. It stands on a site once occupied by a Romanesque church dedicated to Christian child martyrs Justo and Pastor, who were beheaded by the Romans outside Madrid. Although rededicated to San Miguel, the church still bears a monument to the infants. ⏲ *20 min. C/ de San Justo 4.* ☎ *91-548-40-11. www. bsmiguel.es. Free admission. Mon–Sat 10:30am–12:30pm, 7–8:30pm; Sun 9:45am–1:45pm, 6:30–9pm. Metro: Ópera.*

⑭ Puerta Cerrada. The Puerta Cerrada ("closed door") is named after the city's medieval gateway, which stood on this spot until the 16th century. Thieves used to lurk in the shadows, ready to prey on all those who entered; as a

consequence, the gate was usually locked. Now the square is little more than a confluence of streets, but several of the alleys that splinter off here are lined with good restaurants and bars—especially **Calle de Cuchilleros** ("Street of the Knife-sharpeners") and the **Cava Baja** (p 53). ⏲ *10 min. Metro: La Latina.*

⑮ ★★ Plaza del Humilladero. The focus of the obligatory post-Rastro tapas crawl, this square is surrounded by great tapas bars. According to local tradition, it is where the city's patron saint once lived (his master's former home is now the **Museo de los Orígenes**, p 66, ⑥). Next door, the pretty baroque **Capilla de San Isidro** (p 65, ⑤) was built to contain the saint's apparently uncorrupted remains. ⏲ *40 min. Metro: La Latina.*

⑯ ★★ Plaza del Paja. This beautiful square is dominated by the great, domed **Capilla del Obispo.** The "Bishop's Chapel" is one of the finest Renaissance churches in the city, although few Madrileños ever saw the interior because it was closed for 40 years. It was reopened in 2010. Visits must be arranged in advance, but are worth it for a glimpse of the extravagant altar-piece and the splendid marble tombs of Don Francisco de Vargas, councilor for Ferdinand and Isabella, and his family. ⏲ *30 min. To book a visit:* ☎ *91-559-28-74 or e-mail reservascapilladelobispo@arch madrid.es. Metro: La Latina.*

⑰ La Musa Latina. Mouth-watering tapas and a fun and friendly crowd. I prefer it in the early evening; later, it gets packed and service can be frustratingly slow. *Costanilla de San Andrés 12.* ☎ *91-354-02-55. www.lamusalatina.com. Tapas 2.75€–5.75€.* ●

4 The Best Shopping

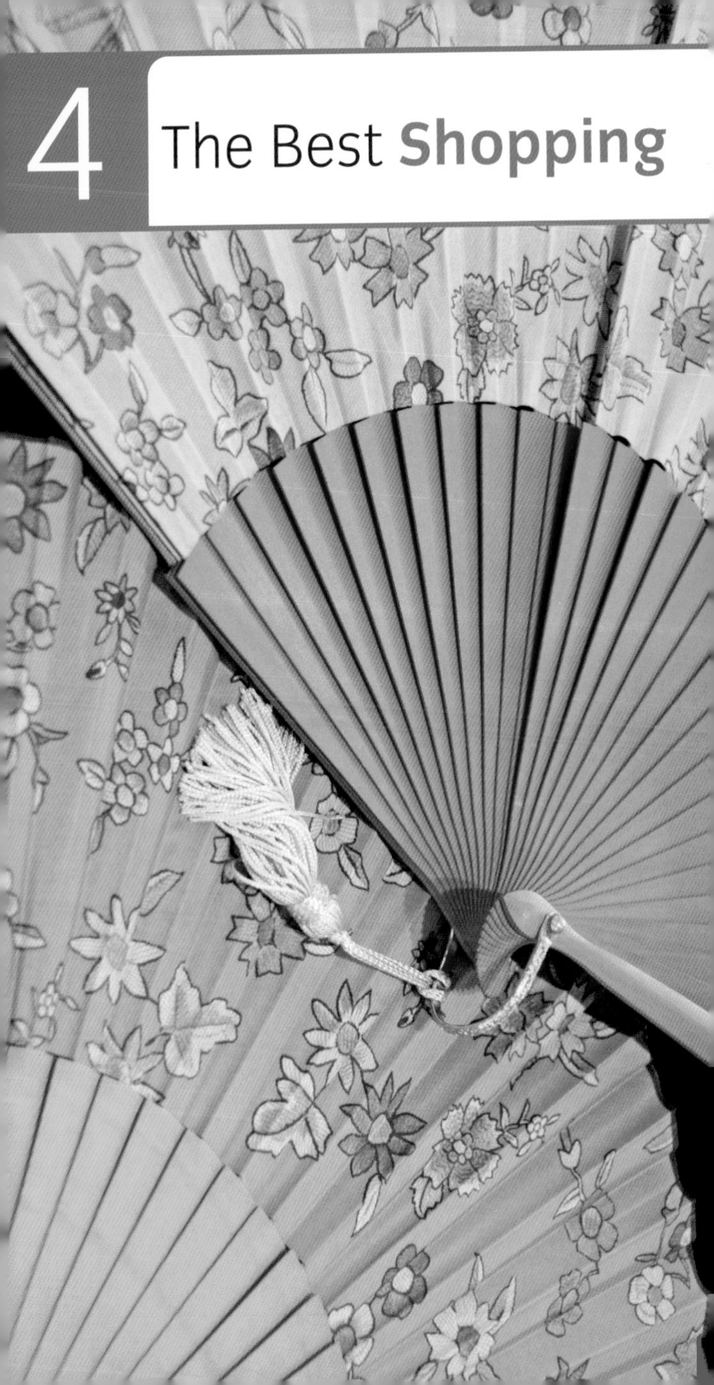

Madrid Shopping

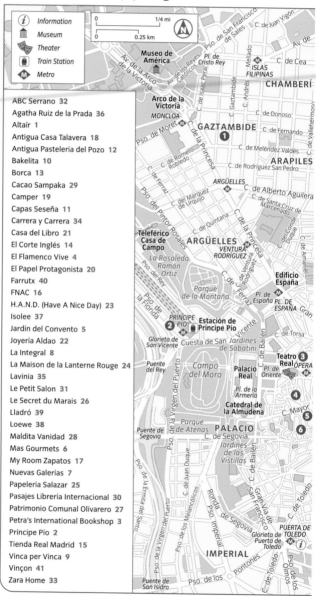

Legend:
- ⓘ Information
- 🏛 Museum
- 🎭 Theater
- 🚉 Train Station
- Ⓜ Metro

0 ——— 1/4 mi
0 ——— 0.25 km

Previous page: Decorative fans.

Shopping Best Bets

Best for **Quirky Gifts**
★ La Integral, *C/ León 25 (p 79)*

Best for **Impulse Buys You Won't Regret (Women)**
★ H.A.N.D., *C/ Hortaleza 26 (p 79)*

Best for **Luxury Leather Goods**
★ Loewe, *C/ Serrano 26 (p 80)*

Best for **Slaves to Design**
★★ Vinçón, *C/ Castelló 18 (p 81)*

Best for **Designer Chocolates**
Cacao Sampaka, *C/ Orellana 4 (p 80)*

Best **Traditional Garment Shop**
★★ Capas Seseña, *C/ de la Cruz 23 (p 81)*

Best **Second-Hand Bookstore**
★★ Petra's International Bookshop, *C/ Campomanes 13 (p 77)*

Best **Flea Market**
El Rastro, *C/ Ribera de Curtidores (p 67)*

Most **Theatrical Boutique**
Agatha Ruiz de la Prada, *C/ Serrano 27 (p 79)*

Best **Spanish Wine Selection**
★ Lavinia, *C/ José Ortega y Gasset 16 (p 80)*

Best **Cakes Made in Convents**
★ Jardín del Convento, *C/ Cordón 1 (p 80)*

Best **Bordello Turned Boutique**
★★ La Maison de la Lanterne Rouge, *C/ Ballesta 4 (p 80)*

Best for **Iberian Ham**
★ Mas Gourmets, *Mercado de San Miguel (p 80)*

Best for **Soccer Fans**
Tienda Real Madrid, *C/ Carmen 3 (p 81)*

Best for **Killer Heels**
Farrutx, *C/ Serrano 7 (p 82)*

Metal robot toys at La Integral.

Madrid Shopping A to Z

Antiques & Art
★ **Nuevas Galerías** CENTRAL MADRID   The street is best known for the Rastro flea market (on Sun), but it's also home to the city's best antiques shops. This site contains 60 individual stores arranged around a courtyard, with a huge range of antiques and bric-a-brac. *C/ Ribera de Curtidores 12.* ☎ *91-520-56-53. Credit cards vary. Metro: La Latina. Map p 74.*

Beauty Products
Le Petit Salon CENTRAL MADRID Treat yourself to a massage or facial at this chic little beauty, or just stop by to pick up their top-of-the-range products. *C/ Almagro 15.* ☎ *91-319-67-51. www.lepetitsalon.es. AE, DC, MC, V. Metro: Alonso Martínez or Rubén Darío. Map p 74.*

★ **Le Secret du Marais** CENTRAL MADRID   This is an Aladdin's cave of beauty products, featuring all the best labels including skincare by Dr. Sebagh and Rodial, make-up by Ellis Faas and Face, and perfumes and candles from Artisan Perfumeur. *C/ Hortaleza 75.* ☎ *91-391-53-54. www.lesecretdumarais.es. MC, V. Metro: Alonso Martínez. Map p 74.*

Books & Music
★ **Altaïr** ARGÜELLES   Superb travel bookstore, with everything from travel guides to hiking maps. *C/ Gaztambide.* ☎ *91-543-53-00. www.altair.es. AE, DC, MC, V. Metro: Argüelles. Map p 74.*

Casa del Libro CENTRAL MADRID This enormous bookstore has a good international section. *Gran Vía 29.* ☎ *91-521-21-13. www.casaddellibro. com. AE, DC, MC, V. Metro: Gran Vía. Map p 74.*

Find English secondhand books at Petra's.

★ **El Flamenco Vive** CENTRAL MADRID   An extensive selection of flamenco CDs, DVDs, and books. *C/ Conde de Lemos 7.* ☎ *91-547-39-17. www.elflamencovive.es. MC, V. Metro: Ópera. Map p 74.*

kids **FNAC** CENTRAL MADRID   The FNAC megastore offers mainstream books and music, plus tickets to all major gigs in the city. It also sells electronic goods from computers to cameras. *C/ Preciados 28.* ☎ *91-595-62-00. www.fnac.es. AE, DC, MC, V. Metro: Gran Vía. Map p 74.*

★ **Pasajes Librería Internacional** CENTRAL MADRID   An excellent international bookstore, with a superb range of titles. *C/ Génova 3.* ☎ *91-310-12-45. www.pasajeslibros.com. MC, V. Metro: Alonso Mártinez. Map p 74.*

★★ **Petra's International Bookshop** CENTRAL MADRID A marvelous, rambling second-hand

Prime Shopping Zones

For all the high-street chains, saunter down the Gran Vía. The pedestrianized **Calle Preciados,** which links Gran Vía with the Puerta del Sol, has the big department store El Corte Inglés (see below) and a huge FNAC (see above). The most upscale shopping neighborhood is **Salamanca,** where Gucci, Chanel, and others gather along the **Calle Serrano.** For funky, offbeat fashion, try Chueca, particularly the **triBall** neighborhood (p 62) and the small streets around the **Plaza de Santa Ana.** The Sunday morning flea market, **El Rastro** (p 67, **10**), has been a Madrid staple for centuries.

bookshop (named after the owner's cat), with a huge selection of books in English and other languages. *C/ Campomanes 13.* ☎ *91-541-72-91. www.petrasbookshop.com. No credit cards. Metro: Ópera or Santo Domingo. Map p 74.*

Ceramics & Porcelain
Antigua Casa Talavera CENTRAL MADRID   This shop specializes in the yellow-and-green ceramics from Talavera, a town south of Madrid that has been making it for centuries. You'll find traditional tiles and tableware with colorful floral designs. *C/ Isabel La Católica 2.* ☎ *91-547-34-17. MC, V. Metro: Callao. Map p 74.*

Antigua Casa Talavera.

Lladró CENTRAL MADRID   Lladró's exquisitely fine porcelain is famous around the world. Their expensive white figurines, tableware, and mirrors are available from this flagship store. *C/ Serrano 6–8.* ☎ *91-435-51-12. www.lladro.com. AE, DC, MC, V. Metro: Serrano. Map p 74.*

Department Stores & Shopping Malls
ABC Serrano SALAMANCA   A smart shopping center in the chi-chi Salamanca neighborhood, this is set in the lavishly tiled former ABC newspaper building. The upscale shops and the rooftop restaurant with a fabulous terrace make it popular with

Fashion & Accessories

kids Agatha Ruiz de la Prada

SALAMANCA   This crazy store with its clashing colors and contrasting patterns has a little bit of everything, from adult fashion to fabrics and goods for the home. I especially like the children's clothes, which are fun and original. *C/ Serrano 27.* ☎ *93-319-05-51. www.agatharuizdela prada.com. AE, MC, V. Metro: Serrano. Map p 74.*

★ H.A.N.D. (Have A Nice Day)

CENTRAL MADRID   I defy anyone to leave empty-handed from this hip, relaxed boutique—the dresses, jackets, and tops are irresistible. *C/ Hortaleza 26.* ☎ *91-429-16-18. www.hand-haveaniceday.es. AE, MC, V. Metro: Antón Martín. Map p 74.*

★ La Integral CENTRAL MADRID

A great selection of fun, retro-chic fashion, accessories, underwear, costume jewelry, stationery, and decorative objects. Bright colors and cool design are key, and I often come here to pick up gifts for friends. *C/ León 25.* ☎ *91-429-16-18.*

Hip boutique H.A.N.D.

"ladies who lunch" and business-people. *C/ Serrano 61 (C/ Castellana 34).* ☎ *91-577-50-31. Metro: Núñez de Balbao or Serrano. Map p 74.*

El Corte Inglés CENTRAL MADRID Spain's largest department store chain sells everything from wine to furniture. You'll also find a restaurant, travel agent, and excellent grocery store. *C/ Preciados 3.* ☎ *91-379-80-00. www.elcorteingles.es. AE, DC, MC, V. Metro: Callao. Map p 74.*

★ Isolee SALAMANCA   A huge, loft-style "lifestyle" store on several floors, this has everything for the urban hipster, from contemporary fashion to interior design (furniture, throws, cushions), plus a beauty bar, deli, and cafe. *C/ Claudio Coello 55.* ☎ *90-287-61-36. www.isolee.com. AE, DC, MC, V. Metro: Sol. Map p 74.*

Príncipe Pío CENTRAL MADRID Set in a beautifully converted 19th-century train station, with all the popular fashion chains. *Paseo de la Florida s/n.* ☎ *91-758-00-40. www. ccprincipepio.com. Metro: Príncipe Pío. Map p 74.*

Príncipe Pío is set in a 19th-century converted train station.

www.laintegral25.com. AE, MC, V.
Metro: Antón Martin. Map p 74.

★★ La Maison de la Lanterne
Rouge CENTRAL MADRID   A
brothel-turned-fashion boutique,
this is one of the biggest successes
in the newly revamped triBall neighborhood. It's a fabulous collection
of fashion, accessories, and decorative objects in a suitably theatrical
setting. C/ Ballesta 4. ☎ 91-310-79-
61. http://lalinternaroja.blogspot.
com/. MC, V. Metro: Gran Vía. Map
p 74.

★ Loewe SALAMANCA   This is
probably the most luxurious of the
upmarket Spanish designers. It
started out in leather goods—and
the shoes and bags are still highly
desirable—but has branched into
high fashion in recent years. C/ Serrano 26. ☎ 91-577-60-56. www.
loewe.es. AE, MC, V. Metro: Serrano.
Map p 74.

★ Maldita Vanidad CENTRAL
MADRID   Glamorous, offbeat fashion in a boudoir-style boutique—
one of several great fashion shops
on this street. C/ Campoamor 3.
☎ 91-319-01-32. MC, V. Metro:
Alonso Martínez. Map p 74.

Flowers
★★ Vinca per Vinca. CENTRAL
MADRID   A florist in the fashionable Santa Ana neighborhood, with
a hot-pink facade, lush plants, and
luscious blooms arranged in original
bouquets. It shares space with
AdHoc, which stocks a great line in
original women's fashion and accessories. C/ León 11. ☎ 91-156-82-23.
www.vincapervinca.es. MC, V.
Metro: Antón Martín. Map p 74.

Food & Drink
★ Antigua Pasteleria del Pozo
CENTRAL MADRID   This pastry
shop opened its doors in 1830 and

has been making the tastiest tradi-
tional treats in the city ever since.
C/ del Pozo 8. ☎ 91-522-38-94.
MC, V. Metro: Sevilla. Map p 74.

Cacao Sampaka CENTRAL MADRID
Here, rich designer chocolates come
in unusual flavors (try them with cin-
namon or rose petals). There's a cafe
attached. C/ Orellana 4. ☎ 93-319-
58-40. www.cacaosampaka.com.
AE, DC, MC, V. Metro: Alonso Martínez. Map p 74.

★ kids Jardín del Convento
CENTRAL MADRID   Sweet treats
made by the nuns and monks of
Spanish convents and monasteries.
C/ Cordón 1. ☎ 91-541-22-99. www.
eljardindelconvento.net. MC, V.
Metro: Ópera. Map p 74.

★ Lavinia SALAMANCA   Spectac-
ular shop, with a superb selection of
Spanish and international wines,
plus books and accessories. They
also offer tastings. There is also a
restaurant, El Espacio Gastronómico.
C/ José Ortega y Gasset 16. ☎ 91-426-
06-04. www.lavinia.com. AE, MC, V.
Metro: Serrano or Rubén Darío. Map
p 74.

★ Mas Gourmets CENTRAL
MADRID   Among the best stalls in
the wonderful Mercado de San
Miguel, with Iberian hams and charcuterie, plus a counter-top bar
where you can try their offerings.
Mercado de San Miguel. ☎ 91-541-
14-14. www.masgourmets.com.
MC, V. Metro: Sol. Map p 74.

★ Patrimonio Comunal
Olivarero CENTRAL MADRID
A shrine to olive oil, with more than
200 varieties of the liquid gold.
C/ Mejia Lequerica 1. ☎ 91-308-
05-05. www.pce.es. MC, V. Metro:
Alonso Martínez. Map p 74.

Gifts & Souvenirs
★ Borca CENTRAL MADRID   This
shop specializes in hand embroidery,

with exquisite *mantillas* (the classic Spanish fringed shawl), tablecloths, and bed linen. A little Spanish will go a long way here, so bring your phrase book. *C/ del Marqués Viudo de Portejos 2.* ☎ *91-523-61-53. AE, DC, MC, V. Metro: Sol. Map p 74.*

★★ **Capas Seseña** CENTRAL MADRID A classic in Madrid, Seseña specializes in the dignified Spanish cape, available in several styles including updated versions for the 21st century. Camilo José Cela wore a cape from this shop when he was awarded the Nobel prize for literature, and photos in the window show bigwigs swathed in elegant folds. *C/ de la Cruz 23.* ☎ *91-531-68-40. www.sesena.com. AE, DC, MC, V. Metro: Sol. Map p 74.*

kids Tienda Real Madrid CENTRAL MADRID Fans of the Merengues ("meringues," for their all-white strips) can pick up official Real Madrid (see box, p 47) merchandise at this central location. There's a bigger shop at the Santiago Bernabéu stadium (p 128). *C/ Carmen 3.* ☎ *91-521-79-50. www. tiendarealmadrid.com. AE, DC, MC, V. Metro: Sol. Map p 74.*

Housewares & Furnishings
★ **Bakelita** CENTRAL MADRID A chic boutique selling vintage furnishings and *objets d'art* from the 20th century. Although some price tags will make you gasp, several pieces are surprisingly affordable. *C/ Cervantes 26.* ☎ *91-429-23-87. www.bakelita.com. AE, DC, MC, V. Metro: Sol. Map p 74.*

★★ **kids Vinçon** CENTRAL MADRID A contemporary design emporium with everything from furnishings to kitchen goods, including lighting and children's toys. *C/ Castelló 18.* ☎ *91-578-05-20. www. vincon.com. AE, DC, MC, V. Metro: Velázquez. Map p 74.*

Zara Home CENTRAL MADRID Affordable interior design, with bedding, lamps, and soft furnishings. This is the biggest Zara Home store in the city, with a special section for Zara Kids Home. *C/ Serrano 88.* ☎ *90-090-03-14. www.zarahome. com. AE, DC, MC, V. Metro: Rubén Darío. Map p 74.*

Stylish vintage furniture at Bakelita.

Jewelry

★ **Carrera y Carrera** SALAMANCA Spain's answer to Tiffany and Cartier (both have shops on this swanky street), Carrera y Carrera is known for bold, contemporary jewelry designs and watches made with precious metals and gems. (Their pieces are regularly seen in the society pages.) Even if the designs are out of your price range, visit just to see the stunning flagship store. *C/ Serrano 76.* ☎ *91-576-64-22. www. carreraycarrera.com. AE, DC, MC, V. Metro: Serrano. Map p 74.*

★ **Joyería Aldao** CENTRAL MADRID This jewelry shop has been going for more than a century, and still preserves its original interior, complete with chandeliers, Oriental carpets, and elegant wooden display cabinets. They sell jewelry and watches by international designers, as well as their own traditional, supremely elegant designs. *Gran Vía 15* ☎ *91-521-69-25. www.aldao joyeros.com. AE, MC, V. Metro: Gran Vía. Map p 74.*

Shoes

kids **Camper** CENTRAL MADRID Quirky and original designs for everyone that meld style and comfort, and have become internationally hip in recent years. One of several branches around the city. *Gran Vía 54.* ☎ *91-547-52-34. www. camper.es. AE, DC, MC, V. Metro: Gran Vía. Map p 74.*

Farrutx SALAMANCA Leather goods—shoes, bags, wallets, belts—for vampish It-girls

and style-conscious men. Prices are reasonable for the quality on offer, but I still sneak off to their sale shop, at Calle Augusto Figueroa 18 in Chueca (☎ 91-532-02-40) to rummage for bargains. *C/ Serrano 7.* ☎ *91-576-94-93. www.farrutx.es. AE, DC, MC, V. Metro: Retiro. Map p 74.*

★ **My Room Zapatos** CENTRAL MADRID A pretty boutique in the style of someone's bedroom, with shoes spilling out of the wardrobe or propped on top of the mirror. Labels include Bruno Premi and Dorotea. *Gran Vía 54.* ☎ *91-547-52-34. www.myroomzapatos.com. MC, V. Metro: Gran Vía. Map p 74.*

Stationery

El Papel Protagonista CENTRAL MADRID Every paper-lover's dream, this is packed with everything from feather-light Chinese silk paper to organic paper goods from Mexico, plus designer stationery by the likes of Vera Wang. *Plaza María Soledad Torres Acosta 2.* ☎ *91-523-42-13. www.elpapelprotagonista. com. MC, V. Metro: Santo Domingo. Map p 74.*

Papelería Salazar CENTRAL MADRID The city's oldest stationery store still preserves its turn-of-the-20th-century facade and wooden cabinets. Come to breathe in the old-world charm and purchase notebooks, pens, and books. *C/ Luchana 7–9.* ☎ *91-446-18-48. www.papeleriasalazar.com. MC, V. Metro: Bilbao. Map p 74.* ●

Real Jardín **Botánico de Madrid (Botanic Gardens)**

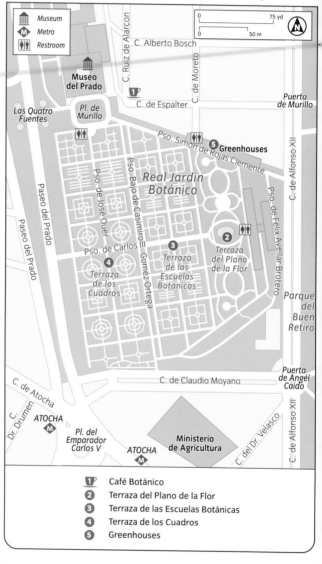

🏛	Museum
Ⓜ	Metro
🚻	Restroom

🏛 **Museo del Prado**

Las Quatro Fuentes

Pl. de Murillo

C. Ruiz de Alarcon

C. Alberto Bosch

C. de Moreto

C. de Espalter

Puerta de Murillo

Pso. Simón de Rojas Clemente

5 Greenhouses

Real Jardín Botánico

Paseo del Prado

Paseo del Prado

Pso. de José Quer

Pso. Bajo de Casimiro

Pso. de Carlos III

Gomez Ortega

3 *Terraza de las Escuelas Botánicas*

4 *Terraza de los Cuadros*

2 *Terraza del Plano de la Flor*

C. de Alfonso XII

Pso. de Félix Avellar Brotero

Parque del Buen Retiro

Puerta de Angél Caído

C. de Claudio Moyano

C. de Atocha

C. Dr. Drumen

Ⓜ **ATOCHA**

Pl. del Emparador Carlos V

Ⓜ **ATOCHA**

Ministerio de Agricultura

C. del Dr. Velasco

C. de Alfonso XII

0 ——— 75 yd
0 ——— 50 m

☕ 1	Café Botánico
2	Terraza del Plano de la Flor
3	Terraza de las Escuelas Botánicas
4	Terraza de los Cuadros
5	Greenhouses

Previous page: Retiro Gardens.

S tep out of the hurly-burly of the city into these beautiful botanic gardens, where birdsong keeps the hum of traffic at bay. Established in 1755, they are laid out in a series of elegant baroque terraces and are particularly inviting in spring, when the flowers come into bloom, and in fall, when the leaves change and drop. START: **Metro to Banco de España. Trip length: 3 hr.**

1 Café Botánico. Just around the corner from the Botanic Gardens, this old-fashioned cafe with a terrace is ideal for a coffee. *C/ Ruiz de Alarcón 27.* ☎ *91-420-23-42. Coffee and a pastry 2.50€.*

2 ★ Terraza del Plano de la Flor. The uppermost terrace, nearest the entrance, is shaded by palms and other trees, with velvety grass fringed with clipped hedges and a charming pond.

3 ★ Terraza de las Escuelas Botánicas. Divided into 12 sections, neatly hedged, and carefully arranged around a dozen stone fountains, the second terrace resembles a baroque *parterre*. A dizzying range of plants is found here, carefully grouped according to their family, and labeled in accordance with their original function—the teaching of botany.

4 ★★ Terraza de los Cuadros. The lowest terrace is also the largest, with ornamental plants, a beautiful rose garden (in bloom from late May through mid-June), a delightful kitchen garden, and—one of my favorites—a section dedicated to medicinal plants. This part of the garden is where Madrileños come to hide themselves away and enjoy a discreet picnic.

5 ★ Greenhouses. Back on the top terrace are the three main greenhouses. The oldest is the graceful 18th-century **Pabellón Villanueva,** used for temporary exhibitions on botanical and

The peaceful Real Jardín Botánico de Madrid.

historical themes. The 19th-century **Graells Greenhouse** is hot and steamy, and contains tropical and aquatic plants including enormous water lilies. The **Exhibition Greenhouse** is dedicated to plants from three different climate types: tropical, temperate, and desert.

Practical Matters

The Botanic Gardens are at Plaza de Murillo 1 (☎ 91-420-30-17; www. rjb.csic.es; Metro: Atocha). Admission costs 2.50€ for adults, 1.25€ students, and free for under-10s. It's open daily 10am to dusk.

Casa **de Campo**

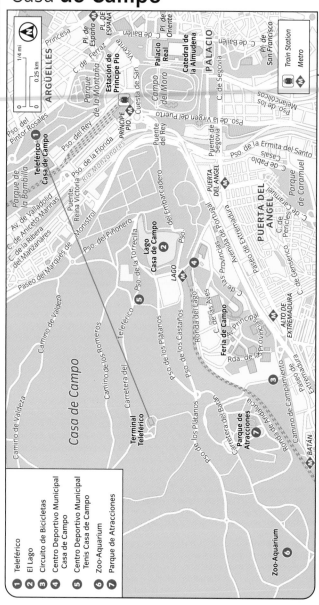

- ➊ Teleférico
- ➋ El Lago
- ➌ Circuito de Bicicletas
- ➍ Centro Deportivo Municipal Casa de Campo
- ➎ Centro Deportivo Municipal Tenis Casa de Campo
- ➏ Zoo-Aquarium
- ➐ Parque de Atracciones

The largest public park in the city, the vast **Casa de Campo** was once a royal hunting ground. Now it's semi-wild, and full of tree-shaded paths, perfect for quiet strolls or mountain biking. There is also a popular lake, as well as tennis courts, the city zoo, and a fun park. START: **Metro to Argüelles, then Teleférico from Parque del Oeste to Casa de Campo, then 15-minute walk. Trip length: 1 day.**

Eating & Drinking in the Casa de Campo

There are numerous fast-food options in the Casa de Campo, from the hot dogs available at the cable car station to the cafes in the zoo and funfair. For more substantial fare, there are restaurants gathered near the lake, but generally the prices are high and the quality is mediocre. I prefer to pick up picnic supplies—either at San Miguel market (p 70) or at the convenient grocery store in El Corte Inglés, C/ de la Princesa 56 (near the Argüelles Metro stop).

1 ★★ kids **Teleférico.** The most entertaining way to reach the Casa de Campo is to take the cable car, which swings over the rooftops at the western end of the city and deposits visitors in the center of the park. Try to go on a clear day, when the views stretch all the way to the distant Sierras. Check the website for opening hours, which change constantly: As a general guide, it's open weekends in winter, daily in summer. It's easier, if rather less fun, to take the Metro to the Lago stop if you want to head directly to the park information center. ⏱ *30 min. Paseo del Pintor Rosales s/n.* ☎ *91-541-11-18. www.teleferico. com. Tickets 3.70€ single, 5.35€ return, free for under-3s. Metro: Argüelles.*

2 ★ **El Lago.** In the southwest corner of the park is a large and extremely popular recreational lake. You can spot it for miles around, thanks to the huge, jetting fountain in the center, which spurts high into the air. There's a useful information pavilion here, with exhibitions on the park's history and on its flora and fauna. It can provide leaflets showing cycling and walking routes,

Take the cable car to Casa de Campo.

The leafy Casa de Campo.

as well as information on guided visits (in Spanish only). *Information center:* ☎ *91-479-60-02. May–Sept 16 10am–2pm and 5–8pm; Sept 17–Apr 9am–2pm and 4–7pm. Metro: Lago.*

❸ **Circuito de Bicicletas.** A circuit specifically tailored to the requirements of mountain-bikers exists within the park. The route begins at the Puerta Dante, near the Batán Metro stop, and takes in a large section of the wildest part of the park. The route is poorly signposted, and the surface frequently changes, from asphalt road to dirt track, so take it slowly the first time you try it out. However, it offers

some spectacular views, and is one of the few places to cycle in Madrid, which is surprisingly bicycle-unfriendly. 🕘 *3 hr. For opening hours, see* ❷.

❹ ★ **Centro Deportivo Municipal Casa de Campo.** This municipal sports center attracts a vast crowd in summer, when the indoor pool is closed and two outdoor pools are opened instead. There is also a children's pool, making this a huge favorite with Madrileño families. It's a shame that there isn't more grass and less cement, but the pools are nonetheless a boon in the searing summer heat. Other facilities include a gym

Bullfighters in the Casa de Campo

If you find yourself strolling through the quieter reaches of the Casa de Campo, you may come across a curious sight: A group of adolescents twirling capes in slow, precise patterns. These are apprentice *toreros* (bullfighters), who attend the prestigious bullfighting school (Escuela Taurina de Madrid) located in the Casa de Campo. Although most of the students are male, a small proportion (roughly 10%) is women. Even if, like me, you disagree with bullfighting, the sight of the slow, dance-like cape movements is mesmerizing.

and sauna, plus special activities and classes. *Paseo Puerta de Angel 7.* ☎ *91-463-00-50. Adults 4.35€, 3.50€ youths 15–20, 2.65€ under-15s. Indoor pool: Early Sept to May Mon–Fri 9:45am–8pm; outdoor pools: Daily 11am–9pm. Metro: Lago or Puerta del Ángel.*

⑤ Centro Deportivo Municipal Tenis Casa de Campo. Practice your backhand at this city-run sports center, with 15 outdoor courts. *Camino Principe 2.* ☎ *91-464-96-17. Adults 5.60€, 4.50€ ages 15–20, 3.40€ under-15s. Hours vary; call in advance. Metro: Lago.*

⑥ Zoo-Aquarium. There are two attractions for the price of one at Madrid's city zoo, which also includes a large aquarium. All the usual favorites are here, from lions and tigers in the zoo to dolphins and penguins in the aquarium. The antics of the crowd-pleasing dolphins (ask for times of shows at the entrance gate) are always hugely enjoyable—although surprisingly short at just 15 minutes. 🕐 *2 hr. Casa de Campo.* ☎ *91-512-37-70.*

www.zoomadrid.com. Adults 19.40€, 15.70€ children 3–7 and seniors, free under-3s. Opening hours vary from week to week, but are approximately daily 11am–6pm in winter, 10:30am–7pm in summer, later at weekends. Closed Jan. Metro: Casa de Campo.

⑦ Parque de Atracciones. You can hear the whoops of delight from this theme park across half of the Casa de Campo. Thrill-seekers will get a rush from some of the scarier rides, which twist through 360° or plunge terrifyingly toward the ground, while the younger (and the more sedate) are well catered for with a host of enjoyable alternatives. *Casa de Campo.* ☎ *91-563-29-00. www.parquedeatracciones.es. Adults 29.90€, children 90–120cm (3–4 ft.) tall 21.50€, free for children under 90cm (3 ft.) tall. Book online for 10% discount. Opening hours vary from week to week, but are approximately Sat–Sun noon–7pm in winter, daily noon–8pm in summer, later at weekends. Metro: Casa de Campo.*

Entrance to Parque de Atracciones.

Parque **del Oeste**

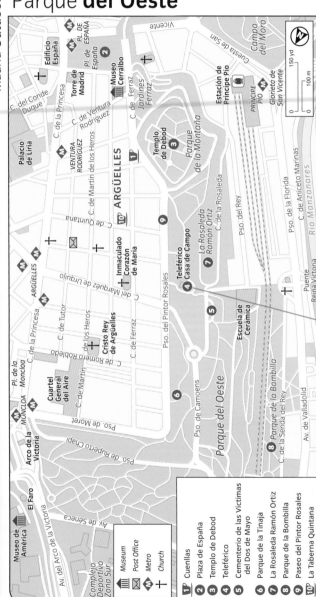

Museum 🏛
Post Office ⊠
Metro ◆
Church ✝

1 Cuenllas
2 Plaza de España
3 Templo de Debod
4 Teleférico
5 Cementerio de las Víctimas del Dos de Mayo
6 Parque de la Tinaja
7 La Rosaleda Ramón Ortiz
8 Parque de la Bombilla
9 Paseo del Pintor Rosales
10 La Taberna Quintana

The undulating, green Parque del Oeste, shaded with tall trees, opened in 1906 and was the city's first, purpose-built public space for relaxation. It is now perhaps best known for its magnificent rose garden, La Rosaleda de Ramón Ortiz, one of the finest in Spain. On summer evenings, the grassy banks fill up with picnickers. START: Plaza de España. Trip length: half-day.

1 Cuenllas. If you're looking for fancy picnic goodies to take into the park, Cuenllas is the answer. Linked to a wonderful tapas bar (on the same street at No. 5), this sells an impressive range of cheeses, wines, oils, spreads, and all kinds of gourmet foodstuffs. *C/ Ferraz 3.* ☎ *91-547-31-33.*

2 Plaza de España. After a quick look at the bronze statues of Don Quijote and Sancho Panza, stride across this large, celebrated, and extraordinarily dull city square toward the shimmering Templo de Debod (see below), just visible in the corner of the Parque del Oeste. *See p 15,* **8**.

3 ★★ kids Templo de Debod. This 4th-century B.C. Egyptian temple once stood on the banks of the Nile, and its serene beauty stands in marked contrast to the ugly modern development around nearby Plaza de España. Fortunately, the gardens in which it sits mark the entrance to the Parque del Oeste, keeping the eyesore apartment blocks at bay. The classic view of the temple, with the huge skies of Madrid stretching behind it, is one of the most amazing spectacles in the city. *See p 21,* **9**.

4 ★★ kids Teleférico. Madrid's enjoyable cable car sways across the western end of the city—and into the huge expanse of the Casa de Campo park—from the cable car

Templo de Debod.

station in the center of the Parque del Oeste. *See p 87,* ❶.

⑤ ★ Cementerio de las Víctimas del Dos de Mayo. This park is very peaceful today, but it's had a surprisingly dramatic history. An arsenal was located here during the Spanish Civil War, where courageous Madrileños came to collect arms in defense of their city (which was the last in Spain to fall to Franco's armies). It was also here that 43 Madrileños who had participated in the citywide uprising were brutally tortured and then shot by Napoleonic troops in the early hours of May 3, 1808. Their corpses were abandoned, but monks gathered the bodies as soon as it was safe to do so and buried them in the nearby cemetery of La Florida, now known as the Cemetery of the Victims of 2nd May. You'll find it in the lower reaches of the park, downhill from the cable car station. The common grave is now marked with a marble monument, and a special service is held here every year on the anniversary of the uprising (May 2). If the cemetery is closed, you can still peek through the gates to admire a tiled reproduction of Goya's masterpiece depicting their execution. ⏲ *30 min.*

⑥ Parque de la Tinaja. Madrid's School of Ceramic Art (Escuela de Arte Cerámica) is located within the park boundaries. Its grounds include the **Parque de la Tinaja,** an attractive, green expanse that sees surprisingly few visitors. The grounds are strewn, rather curiously, with antique train equipment donated by RENFE (Spain's national railway company) and are dominated by a huge, cone-shaped oven, originally built in the 19th century for the production of glass. ⏲ *20 min. Metro: Ventura Rodríguez.*

⑦ ★ La Rosaleda Ramón Ortiz. The undoubted jewel of the Parque del Oeste, La Rosaleda de Ramón Ortiz is a large and outstanding rose garden, scattered with cooling fountains and full of scented bowers and secret corners. It was first laid out in 1956, and annually hosts an important international competition featuring new rose varieties. Most ordinary Madrileños prefer the more fun contest in which they get to vote for whichever

Rose garden fountain.

"El Capricho" de Osuna

Madrid's most beautiful and romantic garden is lost in an urban wilderness of busy ring roads and warehouses on the eastern fringes of the city. **El Capricho de la Alameda de Osuna** is a charming neoclassical palace built as a summer villa by the Duchess of Osuna in the 18th century, and is surrounded by glorious, extensive gardens. The formal French parterre leads into the English garden, scattered with charming follies, and a winding river leads to a delightful boating lake. The gardens are a trek from the city center (a 10-min walk from the Canillejas Metro stop at the end of Line 5, or a taxi-ride) but are worth traveling the distance. They are open at weekends only (until 6pm in winter and 9pm in summer) and admission is free. Picnics are not allowed, but if you're discreet and very careful about tidying up afterward, it's unlikely that anyone will bother you.

bloom they consider the prettiest: People power meets flower power. ⏱ 30 min. *Paseo del Pintor Rosales.* ☎ 91-455-01-29. *Free admission. Daily Nov–Mar 10am–8pm, Apr–Oct 9am–9pm. Metro: Ventura Rodríguez.*

⑧ Parque de la Bombilla. A footbridge at the northern end of the park links the Parque del Oeste with "La Bombi," a smaller park on the other side of the train tracks that is considered an extension of the Parque del Oeste. Grassy expanses are interspersed with terraced walkways, which make for a pleasant stroll. This park hosts the city's traditional celebrations in honor of St. Anthony every June, with parades, dancing, and food stalls. It's also used for an outdoor cinema in summer (June–Aug). You can stroll through the park to the Casa Mingo restaurant-bar (p 104)

or head back uphill to find plenty more places to eat and drink along the Paseo del Pintor Rosales. ⏱ 30 min. *Metro: Moncloa.*

⑨ Paseo del Pintor Rosales. Running along the eastern edge of the park, the Paseo del Pintor Rosales is lined with terrace cafes and restaurants. It's always jam-packed late into the night in summer, when it's one of the few places in the city where a cooling breeze occasionally penetrates the heat. *Metro: Ventura Rodríguez.*

⑩ La Taberna Quintana. A classic neighborhood tavern, with tasty tapas, vermut from the barrel, and a faithful crowd of locals lined up at the bar. *C/ Quintana 17.* ☎ *91-547-31-82. Metro: Argüelles. Beer and a plate of olives 2.50€.*

Parque **del Retiro**

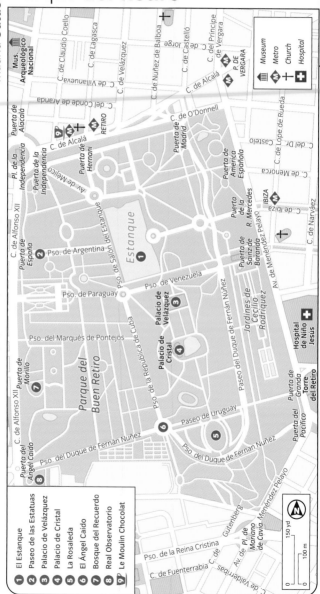

Museum
Metro
Church
Hospital

1 El Estanque
2 Paseo de las Estatuas
3 Palacio de Velázquez
4 Palacio de Cristal
5 La Rosaleda
6 El Angel Caido
7 Bosque del Recuerdo
8 Real Observatorio
9 Le Moulin Chocolat

The Parque del Retiro is one of the world's great city parks—as big as London's Hyde Park and as magical as New York's Central Park. These beautiful gardens—every Madrileño's favorite weekend retreat—are almost all that survive of the Buen Retiro summer palace, a 17th-century royal retreat destroyed by French armies in the early 1800s. START: Metro to Retiro. Trip length: half-day.

1 ★★★ kids **El Estanque.** The centerpiece of the park is this magnificent ornamental lake, dominated by the vast Monument to Alfonso XII, a 19th-century embellishment. The lavish royal barges that featured in elaborate court festivities in the 18th century have given way to bobbing rowboats and the flash of golden carp chasing crumbs.

2 **Paseo de las Estatuas.** A sweeping promenade, flanked on either side by ranks of statues, this is officially called the Paseo de la Argentina del Retiro but more commonly known as the Paseo de las Estatuas ("Statue Promenade"). The statues of every Spanish monarch were originally commissioned by Fernando VI to adorn the royal palace. Fortunately, he was talked out of this flamboyant but graceless gesture, and the redundant statues were relegated to various municipal parks around the city.

3 **Palacio de Velázquez.** This handsome pavilion of red brick, richly decorated with hand-painted tiles, was built in 1883 for an exhibition. It was designed by Ricardo Velázquez Bosco and decorated by the ceramicist Daniel Zuloaga. It's now used by the **Centro de Arte Reina Sofía** museum (p 32, **11**) to host temporary exhibitions. 🕐 *30 min. Paseo Duque de Fernan Núñez (Parque del Retiro).* ☎ *91-573-62-45. www.museo reinasofia.mcu.es. Free admission. May–Sept Mon, Wed–Sat 11am–8pm, Sun and public hols 11am–6pm; Oct–Apr Mon, Wed–Sat 10am–6pm, Sun and public hols 10am–4pm. Closed Tues.*

4 ★★ **Palacio de Cristal.** One of the most striking buildings in Madrid, the fairytale Palacio de Cristal is a glassy pavilion overlooking a small lake. Another of the exhibition pavilions designed by Ricardo Velázquez Bosco in the 1880s, it is

El Estanque ornamental lake.

so delicately constructed that it almost appears to float. It's the perfect spot to spend an afternoon with a picnic and a book. ⏱ *30 min. Paseo Duque de Fernan Núñez (Parque del Retiro).* ☎ *91-574-66-14. www. museoreinasofia.mcu.es. Free admission. May–Sept Mon, Wed–Sat 11am–8pm, Sun and public hols 11am–6pm; Oct–Apr Mon, Wed–Sat 10am–6pm, Sun and public hols 10am–4pm. Closed Tues.*

⑤ ★ **La Rosaleda.** Come in May or June to experience these rose gardens at their finest. Laid out in 1915, the gardens are now one of the most tranquil corners in the Retiro. Tinkling fountains add a romantic touch. ⏱ *30 min.*

⑥ **El Ángel Caído.** Madrid boasts proudly (if less than truthfully) that it is the only capital in Europe to exhibit a statue of the devil. The famous Fallen Angel was created by Ricardo Bellver in 1877 and depicts Lucifer's plummet from heaven as described by Milton in *Paradise Lost.* The city council isn't the only one making up stories: Urban myth relates that the statue stands exactly 666m (2,185 ft.) above sea level and is the focus of dark rituals.

⑦ ★ **Bosque del Recuerdo.** On March 11, 2004, 191 people were killed by terrorist bombs in Madrid. A fortnight later, a special agent was killed by a suicide bomb while attempting to arrest the terrorists. The 192 victims of the attacks are commemorated here in the Forest of Remembrance.

⑧ ★ **Real Observatorio.** The neoclassical Royal Observatory, built in the late 18th century for Carlos III, contains a superb library and a collection of historic astronomical instruments. A full-scale replica of William Herschel's magnificent telescope, installed here in 1805 but then destroyed by Napoleon's troops, is housed in an elegant modern pavilion. Guided visits are in Spanish only. ⏱ *1 hr. C/ Alfonso XII 3.* ☎ *91-506-12-61. www.ign.es/rom/. Adults and children 3 and above 5€, free 2 and under. Visits Fri 4:30pm (5:30pm June–Aug); Sat 10am, noon, 4:30pm (5:30pm June–Aug), Sun 10am, noon.*

☕ **Le Moulin Chocolat.** Pick up a fresh chocolate croissant or a cream-filled éclair this French-style pâtisserie near the Retiro metro stop. *C/ Alcalá 77.* ☎ *91-431-81-45. www.moulinchocolat.com. Snacks 1.50€–4€.* ●

Palacio de Cristal.

Dining Best Bets

Best for a **Gourmet Blow-Out**
★★★ Santceloni *Paseo de la Castellana 577 (p 109)*

Best for **Vermouth from the Barrel**
★ Bodega de la Ardosa *C/ Colón 13 (p 102)*

Best for **Contemporary Tapas**
★★ Le Cabrera *Paseo de la Recoletos 2 (p 107)*

Most **Hip Cafe**
★ Delic *Plaza de la Paja s/n (p 112)*

Best for **Old-Fashioned Tapas**
★ El Mollete *C/ de la Bola 4 (p 106)*

Best **Dining with Views**
★★★ La Mirador del Museo *Paseo del Prado 8 (p 107)*

Best **Outdoor Dining**
Bokado *Avda de Juan de Herrera 2 (p 102)*

Best Place to **See & Be Seen**
★ Be Chic Loft *C/ Valverde 28 (p 102)*

Best for **Kids**
Peggy Sue's American Diner *C/ Belén 5. (p 108)*

Best for **Chocolate con *Churros***
★ Chocolatería San Ginés *Pasadizo de San Ginés 5 (p 111)*

Best for **Your Spanish Grandmother's Cooking**
★ Casa Alberto *C/ Huertas 18 (p 103)*

Best for **Vegetarian Food**
★ La Isla del Tesoro *C/ Manuela Malasaña 3 (p 107)*

Best for **Views of the Plaza Mayor**
Casa Maria *Plaza Mayor 23 (p 104)*

Best **Traditional Tiles**
★ Bocaíto *C/ Libertad 6 (p 102)*

Best for **Romance on a Budget**
Ma Bretagne *C/ San Vicente Ferrer 9 (p 107)*

Best **Rustic Summer Terrace**
★ Casa Mingo *Paseo de la Florida 34 (p 104)*

Best for **Dawdling over Coffee & Newspapers**
★ Café de los Austrias *Plaza Ramales 1 (p 111)*

Best for **Wine & Tapas**
★ Matritum *C/ Cava Alta 16 (p 108)*

Best for **Affordable Avant Garde Cuisine**
★ Restaurante Lúa *C/ Zurbano 85 (p 109)*

Previous page: Cafe del Circulo de Bellas Artes. Below: Chocolatería San Ginés.

Central Madrid Dining

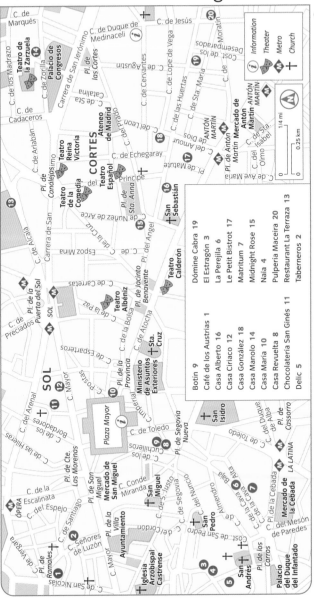

Botín 9
Café de los Austrias 1
Casa Alberto 16
Casa Ciriaco 12
Casa González 18
Casa Manolo 14
Casa Maria 10
Casa Revuelta 8
Chocolatería San Ginés 11
Delic 5

Dómine Cabra 19
El Estragón 3
La Perejila 6
Le Petit Bistrot 17
Matritum 7
Midnight Rose 15
Naia 4
Pulpería Maceira 20
Restaurant La Terraza 13
Taberneros 2

Madrid Dining

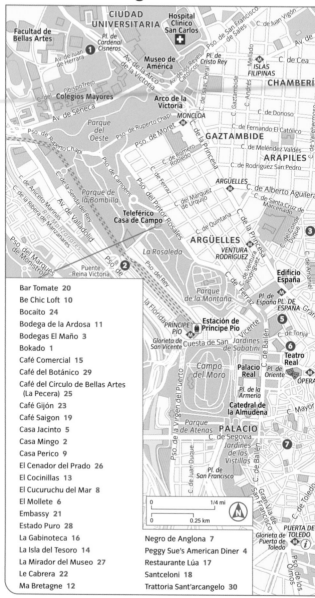

Bar Tomate 20
Be Chic Loft 10
Bocaito 24
Bodega de la Ardosa 11
Bodegas El Maño 3
Bokado 1
Café Comercial 15
Café del Botánico 29
Café del Círculo de Bellas Artes
(La Pecera) 25
Café Gijón 23
Café Saigon 19
Casa Jacinto 5
Casa Mingo 2
Casa Perico 9
El Cenador del Prado 26
El Cocinillas 13
El Cucuruchu del Mar 8
El Mollete 6
Embassy 21
Estado Puro 28
La Gabinoteca 16
La Isla del Tesoro 14
La Mirador del Museo 27
Le Cabrera 22
Ma Bretagne 12

Negro de Anglona 7
Peggy Sue's American Diner 4
Restaurante Lúa 17
Santceloni 18
Trattoria Sant'arcangelo 30

Information
Museum
Theater
Train Station
Metro

Filipinas
C. de Ríos Rosas
RÍOS ROSAS
Pl. de San Juan de la Cruz
Museo Ciencias Naturales ⑰
Murillo
Engracia
C. de Breton de los Herreros
Bermúdez
CANAL
C. de José Abascal
GREGORIO MARAÑÓN ⑱
C. de Fernández de la Hoz
C. de Zurbano
C. de José
ALONSO CANO
⑯
Pl. del Doctor Marañón ⑲
C. de Magallanes
C. de Bravo
C. de Garcia
de Paredes
C. del General Oráa
C. de Viriato
Gta. de Pintor Sorolla
Pso. de General Martínez Campos
Glorieta de Emilio Castelar
C. de Diego
Gta. de Quevedo
C. de Eloy Gonzalo
IGLESIA
C. de Rafael Calvo
CASTELLANA
QUEVEDO
Pl. de Olavide
Pso. de Eduardo Dato
Gta. de Rubén Darío
TRAFALGAR
C. de Santa Engracia
C. de Luchana
RUBÉN DARÍO
C. de Claudio Coello
C. de Lagasca
SAN BERNARDO
C. de Fuencarral
BILBAO
Gta. de Bilbao
C. de Almagro
NÚÑEZ DE BALBOA
C. de José
Gta. de Ruiz Jiménez
C. de Carranza
C. de Sagasta
ALMAGRO
Zurbarán
C. de la Castellana
C. de Serrano
⑭⑮
C. de Fuencarral
C. de Barceló
Pl. de Alonso Martínez
ALONSO MARTÍNEZ
C. de Génova
⑳ ㉑
C. de Ayala
UNIVERSIDAD
C. de San Vicente de Ferrer
⑫
TRIBUNAL
C. de Hortaleza
SERRANO
Pl. de Colón
C. de
Goya
RECOLETOS
C. de Hermosilla
NOVICIADO
⑬
④
Pso. de Recoletos
COLÓN
C. de Bárbara de Braganza
VELÁZQUEZ
C. de San Bernardo
⑪
CHUECA
Biblioteca National
C. Villanueva
C. de Velázquez
C. de Núñez de Balboa
CENTRO
⑨
⑩
C. de Fuencarral
JUSTICIA
㉒
Mus. Arqueológico Nacional
㉓
RETIRO
Vía
Pl. del Callao
C. de Barco
Gran Vía
㉔
BANCO DE ESPAÑA Plaza de Cibeles
Puerta de Alcalá
Alcalá
STO. DOMINGO
CALLAO
Gran Vía
C. de Alcalá
C. de
Pl. de la Independencia
Po. de Salón del Estanque
GRAN VÍA
㉕
Estanque
C. del Arenal
Pl. de la Puerta del Sol
SEVILLA
Museo Thyssen-Bornemisza ㉖
Carrera de San Jerónimo
C. de Montalbán
Po. de Argentina
SOL
Puerta del Sol
SOL
㉗
Paseo del Prado
C. de A. Maura
Pl. de Santa Cruz
CORTES
C. de Felipe
Plaza Mayor
ⓘ
C. de Atocha
C. del Prado
ⓘ
㉘
JERÓNIMOS
Pso. de la República de Cuba
Paso de la República de Cuba
Pl. de Tirso de Molina
C. de las Huertas
Museo del Prado ㉚
Parque del Buen Retiro
TIRSO DE MOLINA
ANTÓN MARTÍN
㉙
LA LATINA
C. de Atocha
Real Jardín Botánico
C. de Alfonso XII
EMBAJADORES
C. de Sta. Isabel
Pl. de Lavapiés
Museo Nacional Centro de Arte Reina Sofía
Pl. del Emperador Carlos V
Pso. de Fernán Núñez
C. de la Ribera de Curtidores
LAVAPIÉS
C. Valencia
Ronda de Atocha
Estación de Atocha
ATOCHA RENFE
Pso. de la Reina Cristina
C. del Casino
ATOCHA
C. de Sta. María de la Cabeza
Av. de la Ciudad de Barcelona
Glorieta de Embajadores
Ronda de Toledo
Pso. de las Acacias
EMBAJADORES
C. de Méndez Álvaro
ACACIAS
PALOS DE MOGUER

Madrid Dining A to Z

★ **Bar Tomate** CENTRAL MADRID *MEDITERRANEAN* A spacious bistro-style restaurant, stylishly decorated in a contemporary rustic style, Bar Tomate serves fresh Mediterranean dishes with a modern twist. Great tapas, but the main dishes (grilled hake with olive tapenade, roast pork) are also good. Best of all are the daily specials: Paella is served on Thursdays. Book ahead. *C/ Fernando el Santo 26.* ☎ *91-702-38-70. Main course 10€–18.50€. AE, DC, MC, V. All day Mon–Sun. Metro: Colón. Map p 100.*

★ **Be Chic Loft** CENTRAL MADRID *CONTEMPORARY SPANISH* This is *the* place to hang out in Chueca, with chic white-on-white decor and cascades of fresh flowers. The cuisine is equally fresh and modern, served as *raciones* (large tapas), which are perfect for sharing. Try the prawn carpaccio, or the foie gras ravioli. I recommend the tasting menu (*menú de degustación*) for 40€. *C/ Valverde 28.* ☎ *91-308-05-70. www.bechic-catering.com. Main course 12€–19.50€. AE, DC, MC, V. Lunch & dinner Tues–Sat. Metro: Gran Vía. Map p 100.*

★ **Bocaíto** CHUECA *TRADITIONAL SPANISH* This traditional eatery, with its colorful tiles and wrought-iron decorative grilles, blends Castilian and Andalucian decor. The tapas are excellent, but you'll also find substantial fare, including grilled meats, stews, and fresh fish. I particularly like the famous *mejime-chas*—mussels topped with béchamel sauce and grilled. *C/ Libertad 6.* ☎ *91-532-12-19. www.bocaito.com. Main course 11.80€–26€. MC, V. Lunch & dinner Mon–Fri, dinner Sat. Closed Aug. Metro: Chueca. Map p 100.*

★ **Bodega de la Ardosa** CENTRAL MADRID *TAPAS* With a century-old facade, huge barrels, and colorful tiles, this is among the most atmospheric of Madrid's bodegas. Try the *salmorejo*—a thick tomato soup served chilled with diced ham and boiled egg. Draft beers are excellent, but on a hot day there's nothing better than an ice-cold vermouth and a plate of olives. *C/ Colón 13.* ☎ *91-521-49-79. www.laardosa.com. Tapas from 1.50€. MC, V. All day Mon–Sun. Metro: Tribunal. Map p 100.*

★ **Bodegas El Maño** CENTRAL MADRID *TAPAS* A classic in the Malasaña neighborhood, this has an appealingly old-fashioned interior, with painted wooden barrels and marble-topped tables. Join the locals with an ice-cold *vermut de grifo* (vermouth from the barrel) or a draft beer, accompanied by a plate or two of their delicious tapas. *C/ de la Palma 64.* ☎ *91-521-50-57. Tapas 1.50€–7.50€. No credit cards. All day Mon–Sat, lunch Sun. Metro: Noviciado. Map p 100.*

Bokado NORTHWEST MADRID *CONTEMPORARY SPANISH* This über-cool restaurant is located in the Museo del Traje (Fashion Museum, p 47, **7**)—ask for a table on the terrace, which overlooks the gardens and fountains. Try hake with clams and Basque-style green sauce. *Pintxos* (Basque tapas, made with slices of French bread with exotic toppings) are served in the adjoining cafe. *Avda. de Juan de Herrera 2.* ☎ *91-549-00-41. www.bokadogrupo.com. Menus 43€ and 50€. AE, MC, V. Lunch & dinner Tues–Sat. Metro: Ciudad Universitaria. Map p 100.*

The cellar dining room of restaurant Botín.

★ **Botín** CENTRAL MADRID *TRADITIONAL SPANISH*   The oldest restaurant in the world (founded in 1725), Botín is located in a cavernous cellar attached to the Plaza Mayor. It's firmly on the tourist trail, but even Madrileños recognize that the star dish—roast suckling pig (*cochinillo asado*)—is outstanding. *C/ Cuchilleros 17.* ☎ *91-366-42-17. www.botin.es. Main course 10.65€– 22€. AE, DC, MC, V. Lunch & dinner daily. Metro: Tirso de Molino. Map p 99.*

★ **Café Saigon** SALAMANCA *VIETNAMESE/ASIAN*   The decor evokes French Indochina, with its carved wooden screens and potted palms. The menu includes Chinese and Thai dishes along with Vietnamese favorites, although spices have been toned for the Spanish palate. Go for the dim sum and follow with duck curry. *C/ Maria de Molina 4.* ☎ *91-563-15-66. www.cafesaigon. es. Main course 11€–20€. AE, DC, MC, V. Lunch & dinner daily. Metro: Gregorio Marañón. Map p 100.*

★ **Casa Alberto** CENTRAL MADRID *TRADITIONAL TAPAS*   With almost 2 centuries of history, the Casa Alberto is a stalwart of Madrid's culinary scene. This is where locals come to relive their grandmother's cooking with delicious, time-honored recipes. Choose from classic tapas such as *croquetas* or meatballs (*albóndigas*) at the bar, or hearty stews and chops in the *comedor*. *C/ Huertas 18.* ☎ *91-429-93- 56. www.casaalberto.es. Tapas from 1.50€, main course 13.50€–16.60€. AE, DC, MC, V. Lunch & dinner Tues– Sat, lunch Sun. Metro: Antón Martín. Map p 99.*

Casa Ciriaco CENTRAL MADRID *TRADITIONAL SPANISH*   Famous bullfighters, writers, and painters once made this their second home—when you've seen the tiled interior and met the courtly waiters, you might do the same. Try all the Madrileño classics, from *callos* (tripe) to *cocido* (pork stew, only on Tues), and the excellent *gallina en pepitoria* (chicken casserole). *C/ Mayor 12.* ☎ *91-548-06-20. Main*

Churros con chocolate *at Casa Manolo.*

course 13€–22€. MC, V. All day
Thurs–Tues. Closed Aug. Metro:
Antón Martín. Map p 99.

Casa González CENTRAL MADRID
TRADITIONAL TAPAS A neighborhood institution, Casa González
has been going since 1931. It's a
charming cross between an anti-
quated deli and bar, and is the ideal
place to try platters of Spanish
cheeses, hams, and cured meats
accompanied by fine wines. If you
like what you sample, products can
be purchased and vacuum-packed
at the deli counter. *C/ León 12.*
☎ *91-429-56-18. Tapas from 2.50–
9€. MC, V. All day Mon–Sun. Metro:
Antón Martín. Map p 99.*

Casa Jacinto CENTRAL MADRID
TRADITIONAL SPANISH Hearty
Castilian cuisine is the draw at this
welcoming tavern with traditional
decoration, including a huge bull's
head. Good *callos* (tripe), a
Madrileño staple, and roast meats
feature, as well as a small selection
of seafood and salads. The *chuletas
de lechal* (lamb chops) and the
stews are always good. *C/ Reloj 20.*
☎ *91-542-67-25. Main course
8.50€–16.50€. MC, V. Lunch & dinner Mon–Sat. Closed Aug. Metro:
Plaza de España. Map p 100.*

Casa Manolo CENTRAL MADRID
TRADITIONAL TAPAS Some of the
finest *croquetas* in the city are
served in this cozy bar behind the
parliament. For a snack, try a delicious *empanada* (small pie filled
with meat or tuna), or try *churros
con chocolate*—fried dough strips
dipped into thick hot chocolate—for
breakfast. For lunch, don't miss the
famous *rabo de toro* (oxtail stew).
C/ Jovellanos 7. ☎ *91-521-45-16.
Tapas from 2.50–9€. MC, V. All day
Tues–Sat, Mon until 5pm. Metro:
Banco de España. Map p 99.*

Casa Maria CENTRAL MADRID
MODERN SPANISH The interior
here preserves its original brick
arches, but the bright walls and
paintings give it a modern feel. The
menu features classic Madrileño
favorites such as stews and roasts,
as well as lighter salads and vegeta-
ble dishes. *Plaza Mayor 23.* ☎ *90-
220-30-25. www.casamariaplaza
mayor.es. Main course 9€–16.50€.
AE, DC, MC, V. All day Mon–Sun.
Metro: Sol. Map p 99.*

★ **Casa Mingo** CENTRAL MADRID
TRADITIONAL SPANISH Built in
1888, this huge, rustic restaurant
has barely changed in a century and
a half. Join the locals at the wooden
tables and tuck into basic tavern

fare, such as hunks of roast chicken served with Asturian cider—poured from shoulder height to retain the fizz. The summer terrace is one of the most popular in the city. *Paseo de la Florida 34.* ☎ *91-547-79-18. www.casamingo.es. Tapas 2€–9.50€. No credit cards. Lunch & dinner daily. Metro: Príncipe Pío. Map p 100.*

Casa Perico CENTRAL MADRID *TRADITIONAL SPANISH* This cluttered, cozy *casa de comidas* has been going since 1942, and is still one of the best places in the old city for traditional Madrileño food. Come for the lentil and pork stews, the lamb chops, or the celebrated *croquetas*. They make their own simple desserts, including a great *flan* (caramel pudding). *C/ Ballesta 18.* ☎ *91-532-81-76. www.casapericomadrid. com. Main course 2.50€–9€. MC, V. Lunch & dinner Mon–Fri, lunch Sat. Metro: Gran Via. Map p 100.*

Casa Revuelta CENTRAL MADRID *TAPAS* This tiny bar is little more than a hole in the wall, with a metal counter-bar, and just three or four tables, but it has a huge reputation for Madrileño favorites such as *callos* (stewed tripe, usually served on Wed and Thurs), *bacalao rebozado* (battered cod fillet) and *albóndigas* (meatballs in tomato sauce). *C/ Latoneras 3 (off Plaza Puerta Cerrada).* ☎ *91-521-45-16. Tapas from 1.50€. All day Mon–Sun. Metro: La Latina. Map p 99.*

Dómine Cabra CENTRAL MADRID *TRADITIONAL SPANISH* Traditional, affordable, and tranquil, this serves reliable Madrileño cuisine in a charming dining room overlooking a plant-filled patio, and is handily set in Santa Ana. Set lunch and dinner menus are bargains at 19€ and 14€, respectively. There's always plenty of choice (the duck is good), and service is attentive. *C/ Huertas 54.*

☎ *91-429-43-65. www.restaurante dominecabra.com. Main course 7.90€–12.90€. MC, V. Lunch & dinner Mon–Sat, lunch Sun. Closed Mon in Aug. Metro: Antón Martín. Map p 99.*

El Cenador del Prado CENTRAL MADRID *MODERN SPANISH* This is the place to treat yourself without breaking the bank. Brightly painted walls contrast with antiques and chandeliers, and service is formal without being stuffy. The seasonal menu might include turbot in a light herb crust, or their famous *patatas a la importancia* (potatoes fried with garlic, parsley, and saffron). *C/ Prado 4.* ☎ *91-429-15-61. Main course 12€–28€. AE, DC, MC, V. Lunch & dinner Mon–Sat. Metro: Antón Martín. Map p 100.*

El Cocinillas CENTRAL MADRID *MEDITERRANEAN* Distressed wooden cabinets and gleaming white linen make this a pretty option for dining in boho Malasaña. The menu takes a twirl around the Mediterrean, with Sicilian pasta, Moroccan couscous, and Provençal salads jostling with Spanish *croquetas* and meatballs. There are usually tasty veggie options too. *C/ San Joaquín 3.* ☎ *91-523-29-60. Main course 9€–16.50€. AE, DC, MC, V. Lunch & dinner Tues–Sat, lunch Sun. Metro: Tribunal. Map p 100.*

El Cucuruchu del Mar CENTRAL MADRID *SEAFOOD* It might seem strange, but the landlocked Spanish capital is famous for its seafood. This place is hugely popular, thanks to its fresh fish (flown in daily), central location, and reasonable prices. The lunchtime *menú del día* (Mon–Fri) is a great deal. It's easy to find: Look for the giant prawn by the door. *Postigo de San Martín 6.* ☎ *91-524-08-41. Main course 9€–26€. MC, V. Lunch Mon, lunch & dinner Tues–Sun. Metro: Callao. Map p 100.*

Try El Mollete for an adventurous range of tapas.

El Estragón CENTRAL MADRID
VEGETARIAN This attractive restaurant overlooks one of central
Madrid's most charming squares.
The tables are scattered over three
levels and the rustic decor is homey
and friendly. Food is healthy and
tasty (dishes include veggie goulash
and a vegetarian paella) and there
are vegan options too. Eat out on
the terrace in summer. *C/ Plaza de
la Paja 21.* ☎ *91-365-89-82. www.
elestragonvegetariano.com. Main
course 7€–13€. MC, V. Lunch &
dinner daily. Metro: La Latina. Map
p 99.*

★ **El Mollete** CENTRAL MADRID
MODERN SPANISH A pleasantly
dated tavern with rustic decor and a
handful of tables, El Mollete serves
an adventurous range of tapas and
raciones. Along with homemade
croquetas and *tortilla*, you might
find caramelized *morcilla* (blood
sausage) or duck *magret* with man-
darin sauce. My favorite is the classic *huevos estrellados*—oven-baked
potatoes and eggs. *C/ de la Bola 4.*
☎ *91-547-78-20. Tapas from 2.50€.
No credit cards. Lunch & dinner
daily. Metro: Ópera. Map p 100.*

★ **Estado Puro** CENTRAL MADRID
CONTEMPORARY TAPAS This glittering fashion hot-spot is run by
celebrity chef Paco Roncero. It's
tucked away in a cellar under the
NH Hotel Paseo del Prado, and is
wildly decorated with retro frescoes
and thousands of traditional flamenco hair-combs. There's also a
terrace during the summer months.
Traditional tapas such as *croquetas*
and *callos* (tripe) are on the menu,
but so are one or two more inven-
tive creations such as the sublime
deconstructed *Tortilla del siglo XXI*
(21st-century omelet). *Plaza Cáno-
vas del Castillo 4.* ☎ *91-573-95-54.
www.tapasenestadopuro.com.
Tapas 8€–25€. AE, DC, MC, V. All
day Mon–Sat, closes 5pm Sun.
Metro: Banco de España. Map p 100.*

★ **La Gabinoteca** CENTRAL
MADRID *CONTEMPORARY TAPAS*
This relaxed loft-style restaurant is a
modern spin on the traditional tavern. Contemporary versions of classic Madrileño tapas include a
deconstructed tortilla served in a
glass with a cod foam, and

*The terrace restaurant at the Thyssen
museum, La Mirador.*

the fabulous *bocata de calamares* (prepared with baby squid). The food, like the decor, is served with a light, playful touch. *C/ Fernández de la Hoz 53.* ☎ *91-399-15-00. www. lagabinoteca.es. Tapas 1.85€– 6.80€. AE, DC, MC, V. Lunch & dinner Mon–Fri, dinner Sat. Metro: Gregorio Marañón. Map p 100.*

★ **kids La Isla del Tesoro** MALA-SAÑA *VEGAN* A charming vegan restaurant, with a dining room decorated like a beach bar in the Caribbean, this serves more imaginative food than most of Madrid's veggie restaurants. Each day, the menu offers the cuisine from a different country, so you might find a seitan couscous, Thai curry, or wild mushroom pasta. *C/ Manuela Malasaña 3.* ☎ *91-593-14-40. www.isladel tesoro.net. Main course 6.50€– 12.50€. AE, MC, V. Lunch & dinner daily. Metro: Bilbao. Map p 100.*

★★★ **La Mirador del Museo** CENTRAL MADRID *MODERN SPANISH* Many of Madrid's restaurants close down during August but this sublime terrace restaurant, on the roof of the Thyssen museum, is *only* open in summer. The food can barely compete with the extraordinary views, which encompass most of the old center. It's truly breathtaking. Book well in advance. *Paseo del Prado 8.* ☎ *91-429-27-32. www. museothyssen.org. Main course 15€–30€. AE, MC, V. Dinner Tues– Sun. Closed Sept–June. Metro: Banco de España. Map p 100.*

La Perejila CENTRAL MADRID *TAPAS* An Andalucian-style tapas bar on buzzy Cava Baja, this has fun, kitsch flamenco decoration, and a blackboard filled with specials. If you're only in the mood for a snack, go for the *tostadas*—a big slice of toasted country bread with all kinds of delicious toppings. *C/ Cava Baja 25.* ☎ *91-364-28-55. Tapas 4.50€– 12€. MC, V. Lunch & dinner Mon– Sat, lunch Sun. Metro: La Latina. Map p 99.*

★★ **Le Cabrera** CENTRAL MADRID *CONTEMPORARY SPANISH* This has been one of the most talked-about places in town since it opened in 2010. Award-winning chef Sergi Arola and Ben Bensoussan are behind the exquisite *raciones* on offer in the gastro-bar upstairs, with contemporary versions of Spanish classics such as *croquetas* as well as more exotic fare like oyster ceviche. *Paseo de Recoletos 2.* ☎ *91-319-94-57. www. lecabrera.com. Tapas 4€–20€. AE, DC, MC, V. Lunch & dinner Tues–Sat, until 2am Fri–Sat. Metro: Colón. Map p 100.*

★ **Le Petit Bistrot** CENTRAL MADRID *FRENCH* A little corner of Paris in Madrid, this cozy wood-paneled restaurant is always full, thanks to its good French food and very reasonable prices. Specialties include the onion soup, *magret* of duck, and steak tartare. *Plaza de Matute.* ☎ *91-429-62-55. www.le petitbistrot.net. Main course 11€– 20€. MC, V. Lunch Mon, lunch & dinner Tues–Sat. Metro: Antón Martín. Map p 99.*

Ma Bretagne CENTRAL MADRID *FRENCH* This intimate, candle-lit creperie is perfect for a romantic supper. Starters include platters of cheeses, charcuterie, pâtés, and good salads, followed with Breton-style crepes with a range of fillings. It's popular with a young, student crowd, who come for the atmosphere and the low prices. *C/ San Vicente Ferrer 9.* ☎ *91-531-77-74. Main course 4.50€–7.50€. Dinner 8:30am–1am. Metro: Tribunal. Map p 100.*

Midnight Rose bistro in the Me Madrid hotel.

★ **Matritum** CENTRAL MADRID *TAPAS* Small, stylish, and extremely popular, Matritum offers a wide and well-chosen wine selection accompanied by gourmet tapas. It's a good place to try wines from Spain's emerging boutique wineries. The staff is usually happy to give advice, but be here on the dot at 8:30pm if you want a seat. *C/ Cava Alta 16.* ☎ *91-528-36-62. www.matritum.es. Main course 9€–20€. MC, V. Lunch only Mon–Wed, lunch and dinner Thurs–Sun. Metro: Lavapiés or Antón Martín. Map p 99.*

Midnight Rose CENTRAL MADRID *FUSION* Inside the ultra-fashionable Me Madrid hotel (p 141) is one of the hottest dining spots in town. The burnished gold-and-black decor provides a glitzy setting for the fashion pack, who come less to enjoy the original fusion cuisine than to see and be seen. The kitchen is open until midnight, making it an excellent locale for late-night dining. *Plaza de Santa Ana 14.* ☎ *91-701-60-20. www.midnightrose.es. Main course 9€–26€. AE, MC, V. Lunch & dinner daily. Metro: Sol. Map p 99.*

Naïa CENTRAL MADRID *MODERN SPANISH* A relaxed modern bistro with eclectically mismatched furnishings and a chill-out zone, Naïa has a fantastic terrace on a charming square. Dine on specialties such as Santoña anchovies served with cherry and tomato *pisto*, or tuna tartare with *aguacate* ceviche. Finish up with the indulgent rum and lime sorbet. *Plaza de la Paja 3.* ☎ *91-366-27-83. www.naia restaurante.com. Main course 12€–19.50€. AE, MC, V. Lunch & dinner daily. Closed Mon in winter. Metro: La Latina. Map p 99.*

Negro de Anglona CENTRAL MADRID *MODERN MEDITERRANEAN* With its flamboyant, neo-baroque decoration in bold black and white, and set in a converted 18th-century *palacete*, this place attracts celebs and the fashion pack. The food is well executed, with dishes like venison with chestnuts, or salmon in a champagne sauce. *C/ Segovia 13.* ☎ *91-366-37-53. www.negrode anglona.com. Main course 9.50€–20€. AE, DC, MC, V. Dinner Tues–Fri, lunch & dinner Sat–Sun. Metro: La Latina. Map p 100.*

kids Peggy Sue's American Diner CENTRAL MADRID *NORTH AMERICAN* Children of all ages will love this shiny pink, 1950s-style diner—with its jukebox and chrome counter, it's a step back in time. The hot dogs, burgers, fries, and milkshakes are made on the spot in the open kitchen. Make sure you book ahead because it's very small. One of six branches throughout the city. *C/ Belén 5.* ☎ *91-308-30-93. www. peggysues.es. Main course 4.95€– 6.45€. MC, V. Dinner Mon–Fri, lunch & dinner Sat–Sun. Metro: Chueca. Map p 101.*

Pulpería Maceira CENTRAL MADRID *NORTHERN SPANISH* This tiny restaurant specializes in dishes from Galicia, which is celebrated for its seafood. The most typical Gallego dish is *pulpo* (octopus), served here in the classic style with piquant tomato and paprika sauce. Dishes are perfectly paired with Galician Albariño wines. There's another branch at C/ Huertas 66. *C/ Jesús 7.* ☎ *91-429-15-84. Tapas from 2.50€, raciones from 6.95€. No credit cards. Lunch & dinner Tues–Sat. Metro: Antón Martín. Map p 99.*

★★★ Restaurant La Terraza CENTRAL MADRID *CONTEMPORARY SPANISH* A high-end restaurant in the historic casino, this is the most glamorous place in town.

Award-winning chef Paco Roncero creates some of the most exciting contemporary cuisine in the city, with liberal use of foams and deconstructed dishes in the manner of his teacher, the legendary Ferran Adriá. Dress up, and dazzle your palate. *C/ Alcalá 15.* ☎ *91-532-12-75. www. casinodemadrid.es/en. Main course 36€–75€, tasting menu 110€. AE, MC, V. Lunch & dinner Mon–Fri, dinner Sat. Closed Aug. Metro: Sevilla. Map p 99.*

★ Restaurante Lúa CENTRAL MADRID *MODERN SPANISH* Tradition meets avant garde at this discreetly elegant restaurant. It offers three menus, one of which includes wine pairings, chosen from a short list of dishes that changes each week. These might include a langoustine ceviche with scallops and wakami, or fresh hake with red Thai rice. *C/ Zurbano 85.* ☎ *91-395-28-53. www.restaurantelua.com. Set menus 31€ (lunch only Mon–Fri), 47€, 72€. AE, DC, MC, V. Lunch & dinner Mon–Sat. Metro: Gregorio Marañón. Map p 101.*

The relaxed, modern Naïa bistro.

Café Gijón.

★★★ **Santceloni** CENTRAL MADRID *CONTEMPORARY SPANISH* Head chef Santi Santamaria is one of the finest chefs in Spain: His menu changes with the season but might include perfectly tender lamb with eggplant and olives, or Navarrese asparagus with a hazelnut sabayon. Opt for the *menú gastronomico* (142€) or the *Gran Menú* (177€) for an unforgettable gastronomic treat. *Paseo de la Castellana 577.* ☎ 91-210-88-40. www.restaurante santceloni.com. Main course 37€– 65€. AE, DC, MC, V. Lunch & dinner Mon–Fri, dinner Sat. Closed Aug, Easter week. Metro: Gregorio Mara-ñón. Map p 101.

Taberneros CENTRAL MADRID *TAPAS* This attractive modern tavern is another reliable option for fine wines and excellent tapas. It's worth getting here early to secure a table. An extensive wine list, a knowledgeable staff happy to make recommendations, surprisingly creative food, and reasonable prices make this a sound choice. *C/ Santiago 9.* ☎ 91-542-21-60. www.

restaurantetaberneros.es. Main course 10€–25€. MC, V. Lunch & dinner Tues–Sun. Metro: Ópera. Map p 99.

kids Trattoria Sant'arcangelo CENTRAL MADRID *ITALIAN* This attractive, light-filled trattoria is a handy option if you're in the vicinity of the Prado. The lengthy menu includes all the Italian favorites from pasta to pizza, as well as salads and carpaccio. It's a good place to bring children, with something to keep even the fussiest eaters happy. *C/ Moreto 15.* ☎ 91-369-10-93. www.trattoriasantarcangelo.com. Main course 8.50€–11.20€. MC, V. Lunch & dinner daily. Metro: Gran Vía. Map p 101.

Cafes
★ **Café Comercial** CHUECA *CAFE* This battered and old-fashioned cafe opened in 1887, and the original revolving door still functions perfectly. With its marble-topped tables and wooden chairs, it is the perfect setting for *tertulias* (the discussion groups that Madrileños love), as

well as a local chess club. It's especially good for breakfast. *C/ Glorieta de Bilbao 7.* ☎ *91-521-56-55. Main course 7.50€—12€. MC, V. All day Mon–Sun. Metro: Banco de España. Map p 101.*

kids Café del Botánico CENTRAL MADRID *TRADITIONAL CASTILIAN* Near the Botanic Gardens and the Prado, this charming and elegant cafe has a minuscule *comedor* (dining room) where you can tuck into tapas and traditional dishes such as bean stew with chorizo, or *cocido* (the classic Madrileño stew). It has a great little terrace (although you'll be lucky to find a place). *C/ Ruiz de Alarcón 27.* ☎ *91-420-23-42. Main course from 8€. MC, V. All day Mon–Sun. Metro: Banco de España. Map p 101.*

★★ **kids Café del Círculo de Bellas Artes (La Pecera)** CENTRAL MADRID *CAFE* This elegant 1920s' cafe is in an Art Deco building, with swooping lines and huge picture windows. You can snack on simple sandwiches or tapas, or go

Daytime cafe Delic turns into a cocktail bar at night.

for the well-priced lunchtime *menú del día*. I also like to come here mid-afternoon, when you can often have the place all to yourself—sink into a sofa with a good book. *C/ Marqués de Casa Riera 2.* ☎ *91-360-54-00. www.circulobellasartes.com. Main course 10€—15€. AE, DC, MC, V. All day Mon–Sun. Metro: Banco de España. Map p 101.*

Chocolatería San Ginés.

★ **Café de los Austrias** CENTRAL MADRID *CAFE* The marble columns and worn gilt mirrors give the place plenty of battered charm, particularly in winter; in summer, pull up a chair on the small terrace. The menu covers all bases, with a good selection of meat, fish, and pasta dishes, and there is also a reasonably priced *menú del día* served at weekday lunchtimes. *Plaza Ramales 1.* ☎ *91-559-84-36. www.cafedelosaustrias.com. Main course 7€—12€. AE, MC, V. All day Mon–Sun. Metro: Ópera. Map p 99.*

Café Gijón CENTRAL MADRID *CAFE* Founded in 1888, this was once Madrid's most famous literary cafe (although Hemingway thought it "full of show-offs"). Now favored by smart, older ladies, besuited businessmen, and tourists in search of its romantic past, the red-and-gold Gijón is still a fine spot for mid-afternoon coffee and cake served by aproned waiters. Main meals also available. *C/ Paseo de Recoletos 21.* ☎ *91-521-54-25. www.cafegijon. com. Main course 10€—15€. AE, DC, MC, V. All day Mon–Sun. Metro: Banco de España or Colón. Map p 101.*

★ kids **Chocolatería San Ginés** CENTRAL MADRID *CAFE* Possibly the most famous of Madrid's chocolaterías, this café was established in 1894 and has an enviable reputation for its *churros con chocolate*, Freshly prepared, and light as air,

the long, deep-fried dough strips are utterly delicious. There are a couple of tables outside, or you can eat in the traditional tiled interior. *Pasadizo de San Ginés 5 (off C/ Arenal).* ☎ *91-365-65-46. Hot choc & churros from 3.50€. No credit cards. All day Mon–Sun. Metro: Ópera or Sol. Map p 99.*

★ kids **Delic** CENTRAL MADRID *CAFE* By day a relaxed cafe, and by night a buzzy cocktail bar, Delic is the most stylish of numerous cafes on the lovely Plaza de la Paja. Snack on sandwiches and interesting salads, or tuck into cakes (the carrot cake is the best I've tasted in Spain). Kids can run around the square, while their footsore parents chill out on the terrace. A gem. *Plaza de la Paja s/n.* ☎ *91-364-54-50. Main course 8€—13€. MC, V. All day Tues–Sun, evenings only Mon. Metro: La Latina. Map p 99.*

Embassy CENTRAL MADRID *CAFE* Another of Madrid's classic traditional cafes, this is *the* place to come for afternoon tea. The range of teas and hot chocolates is served with cakes, elegant little sandwiches, and pastries. Join the immaculately coiffed Salamanca ladies and their miniature dogs out on the splendid summer terrace. *Paseo Castellana 12.* ☎ *91-435-94-80. Main course 10€—15€. AE, DC, MC, V. All day Mon–Sun. Metro: Serrano or Colón. Map p 101.* ●

7 The Best
Nightlife

Madrid Nightlife

(i)	Information
🏛	Museum
🎭	Theater
🚇	Train Station
Ⓜ	Metro

Previous page: Chicote.

Nightlife Best Bets

Best for **Old-World Atmosphere**
★ Cervecería Alemana, *Plaza de Santa Ana 6 (p 117)*

Best **Place to Meet the Next Pedro Almodóvar**
Anjelika Cinema Lounge Café, *C/ Cava Baja 24 (p 117)*

Best **Rooftop Views**
★ La Terraza (Hotel Urban), *Carrera de San Jerónimo 34 (p 119)*

Best for **People-Watching**
★ The Penthouse (Me Madrid), *Plaza de Santa Ana 14 (p 119)*

Best for **Classic Cocktails**
★ Museo Chicote, *Gran Vía 12 (p 119)*

Best for **Oysters & Champagne**
★★ Glass Bar (Hotel Urban), *Carrera de San Jerónimo 34 (p 119)*

Best **Rooftop Hideaway**
★★ Gaudeamus, *C/ Tribulete 14 (p 118)*

Best **triBall Hangout**
★★ Santamaría, *C/ Ballesta 6 (p 118)*

Best **Place to Chill Out**
★ Areia, *C/ Hortaleza 92 (p 117)*

Best **Mega Nightclub Venue**
Macumba, *Plaza de la Estación de Chamartín s/n (p 120)*

Best **Original 1980s Bar**
★ La Vía Láctea, *C/ Velarde 19 (p 118)*

Best for **Couples Over 30**
★★ El Jardín Brugal, *Paseo de Recoletos 92 (p 118)*

Best for **Singles**
★ El Perro de la Parte de Atrás del Coche, *C/ Puebla 15 (p 120)*

Best **Gay Party Night**
★ Ohm at Sala Bash, *Plaza del Callao 4 (p 120)*

Most **Romantic Terrace**
★ Belmondo, *C/ Caños Viejos 3 (p 118)*

Best **Place to Catch Up With Friends**
★★ Dos Gardenias, *C/ Santa María 13 (p 117)*

The Penthouse is a great place for people-watching.

Madrid Nightlife A to Z

The century-old Cerveceria Alemana.

Bars & Pubs

Anjelika Cinema Lounge Café
CENTRAL MADRID Part video club
(over 3,000 titles) and part cafe-bar,
this mellow spot serves tapas,
snacks, and cocktails late into the
night. Hang out with Madrid's young
intellectuals, and join in with the
organized talks and debates.
C/ Cava Baja 24. ☎ *91-366-04-94.*
www.angelika.es. Tapas from 1.50€.
Metro: Latina. Map p 114.

★ **Areia** CENTRAL MADRID Sink
onto one of the low sofas piled high
with cushions, and enjoy the soft
lighting, silk drapes, and chilled-out
electronica, lounge, and world
music from guest DJs. Areia serves
fusion food and is open all day.
C/ Hortaleza 92. ☎ *91-310-03-07.*
www.areiachillout.com. Metro:
Alonso Martínez. Map p 115.

★ **Cerveceria Alemana**
CENTRAL MADRID This century-
old, wood-paneled tavern hasn't
changed since Hemingway once

propped up the bar. Brisk waiters in
long white aprons bring you excellent beer accompanied by good
tapas. It's touristy but there's a
faithful local clientele too. *Plaza de*
Santa Ana 6. ☎ *91-429-70-33.*
Metro: Sol. Map p 115.

★★ **Dos Gardenias** CENTRAL
MADRID Perfect for a romantic
tête-à-tête, or a catch-up with
friends, this laidback cafe-bar is
filled with vintage furnishings and
cozy nooks. The music never gets
too loud and the vibe is upbeat and
friendly. *C/ Santa María 13.*
☎ *62-700-35-71. Metro: Antón*
Martín. Map p 115.

★ **El Imperfecto** CENTRAL
MADRID One of the most original
cafe-bars in town, with a quirky mix
of old and new furnishings and a terrace on a sweet little square. Good
for everything from afternoon coffee to late-night cocktails. *Plaza*
Matute 2. ☎ *91-366-72-11. Metro:*
Sol. Map p 115.

★ **El Jardín Brugal** CENTRAL MADRID This summer-only outdoor bar in the Casa de América boasts huge apple-green sunshades with curving benches designed by Héctor Ruiz. Caribbean cocktails, DJs, and live Latin jazz make it a perfect choice for chilling out on hot summer nights. *Paseo de Recoletos 92.* ☎ *91-595-48-00. www.casamerica.es. Metro: Banco de España. Map p 115.*

★★ **Gaudeamus** CENTRAL MADRID This eyrie-like bar offers amazing views over the higgledy-piggledy rooftops of Lavapiés. Tuck into tapas or dinner (book well in advance for a table), or just soak up the views over an ice-cold beer. *Edificio Escuelas Pías, C/ Tribulete 14.* ☎ *91-528-25-94. www.gaudeamus cafe.com. Metro: Lavapiés. Map p 115.*

★ **La Vía Láctea** CENTRAL MADRID A veteran of the *Madrileño Movida* (the countercultural movement that exploded after Franco's death), this is one of the city's oldest haunts. A new generation of artsy, alternative types hangs out under the vaulted ceilings, completely covered in old movie, theater, and concert posters. *C/ Velarde 19.* ☎ *91-446-75-81. www.lavialactea.net. Metro: Bilbao or Tribunal. Map p 115.*

★ **Le Cock** CENTRAL MADRID An upscale, tranquil bar where you can lounge on sofas and sip a well-mixed cocktail. Comfortable without being stuffy, and popular without being too fashionable, it's a great place to while away an hour or two in the early evenings. Later on and at weekends, the music and clientele liven up. *C/ de la Reina 16.* ☎ *91-532-28-26. www.barcock.com. Metro: Gran Vía or Sevilla. Map p 115.*

★ **Maluca** CENTRAL MADRID There aren't too many places in Madrid that will serve you a fresh strawberry daiquiri, but stylish Maluca always comes through. It's one of the smallest bars on this busy, bar-lined street, and it's one of my favorites for starting a long Madrid night on the town. *C/ Calatrava 16.* ☎ *91-356-09-96. Metro: La Latina. Map p 114.*

★★ **Santamaría, La Coctelería de Al Lado** CENTRAL MADRID This chic little cocktail bar in the ultra-fashionable triBall neighborhood has a vintage bar, wooden floors inset with tiles, and long, cushioned benches. Jazzy tunes provide a mellow soundtrack, and there's a great range of cocktails (try the Santamaria—champagne, strawberries, and vodka). It's a little quieter midweek. *C/ Ballesta 6. No phone. Metro: Gran Vía. Map p 115.*

Cocktail Lounges

★ **Belmondo** CENTRAL MADRID A tree-shaded summer terrace under the viaduct arches, expertly mixed cocktails, and a

Glass Bar at Hotel Urban.

La Terraza at Hotel Urban.

spectacular interior (check out the ceiling over the bar) have made this one of the city's hottest addresses. *C/ Caños Viejos 3.* ☎ *91-366-30-13. www.belmondococktails.com. Metro: La Latina. Map p 114.*

★ **Bodegas Rosell** CENTRAL MADRID Colorfully tiled scenes of happy drinkers adorn this old-fashioned *bodega*, very near Atocha station, where you can enjoy a huge selection of wines, chilled *vermut* from the barrel and tasty tapas. *C/ General Lacy 14.* ☎ *91-467-84-58. www.bodegasrosell.es. Metro: Palos de la Frontera. Map p 115.*

★★ **Glass Bar (Hotel Urban)** CENTRAL MADRID It doesn't get much cooler than this: The ultra-slick Hotel Urban's oyster bar is made entirely of glass, from the huge windows to the tables and chairs. Not the place for shrinking violets, this is all about looking good and being seen. Shine up those Manolos. *Carrera de San Jerónimo 34.* ☎ *91-787-77-70. www. derbyhotels.com/en/hotel-urban/. Metro: Sevilla. Map p 115.*

★ **La Terraza (Hotel Urban)** CENTRAL MADRID The Hotel Urban's rooftop bar is the place to be when summer arrives. Sip a cocktail under the stars, as DJs spin mellow sounds. There are just as

many people showing off up here as at the Glass Bar downstairs, but the feel is more relaxed. *Carrera de San Jerónimo 34.* ☎ *91-787-77-70. www. derbyhotels.com/en/hotel-urban/. Metro: Sevilla. Map p 115.*

★ **Museo Chicote** CENTRAL MADRID Countless icons of the 20th century, including Ava Gardner and Frank Sinatra, passed through the doors of Chicote, Madrid's first and most celebrated cocktail club. Its elegantly preserved Art Deco decor makes it a special place for a drink. Different DJs every night crank up the chilled-out lounge music later on, when a younger crowd appears. *Gran Vía 12.* ☎ *91-532-67-37. www.museo-chicote.com. Metro: Gran Vía. Map p 115.*

★ **The Penthouse (Me Madrid)** CENTRAL MADRID Beloved by Madrileño fashionistas, the rooftop bar at the ultra-stylish Me Madrid hotel is one of the city's favorite hangouts. Swoop up in the private lift to join the *gente guapa* (beautiful people) for cocktails, music, and views over the old city. There's a great Sunday brunch, where you're bound to spot the odd celebrity. *Plaza de Santa Ana 14.* ☎ *91-701-60-00. www.memadrid.com/The Penthouse.html. Metro: Sol. Map p 115.*

Dance Clubs

★ **Charada** SALAMANCA This gorgeous "retro-futurist" club is where the young fashion crowd hangs out. Expect the latest electro-pop from international DJs. *C/ La Bola 13.* ☎ *91-758-56-85. www. charadaclubdebaile.com. Cover 15€ includes drink. Metro: Santo Domingo. Map p 114.*

★ **El Perro de la Parte de Atrás del Coche** CENTRAL MADRID Besides the weirdest of names ("The Dog from the Back Part of the Car"), this basement dive is one of the hippest club-cum-live music venues, with a slick, alternative crowd. Eclectic sounds from soul and funk to electronica will have you dancing until dawn. *C/ Puebla 15.* ☎ *91-521-03-25. Cover 8€ includes drink. Metro: Callao. Map p 115.*

Macumba NORTH MADRID This huge club has the city's finest sound system and hosts several top club nights. Danzoo, on Saturday nights, attracts the best international DJs and is currently the top night in town. The Sunday morning "after-party," Space of Sound, is legendary (winter only). *Plaza de la Estación de Chamartín s/n.* ☎ *91-506-02-56. Cover 10€–20€ usually includes drink. Metro: Chamartín. Map p 115.*

Gay & Lesbian Bars/Clubs

Café Antic CENTRAL MADRID A classic in Chueca, the main gay neighborhood in central Madrid, this pretty cocktail bar, with its over-the-top baroque decor, hushed corners, and candlelight, is perfect for romantic trysts or just a conversation. The clientele is largely, but not exclusively, gay. *C/ Hortaleza 4. No phone. Metro: Gran Vía. Map p 115.*

Fulanito de Tal CENTRAL MADRID This friendly disco-bar is on two levels and hosts everything from fashion shows to live music. It's a fun, mixed crowd—gay, lesbian, and gay-friendly. *C/ Conde de Xiquena 2.* ☎ *91-531-01-32. www. fulanitadetal.com. Metro: Chueca. Map p 115.*

★ **Ohm at Sala Bash** CENTRAL MADRID Sala Bash is a massive club in the city center. The biggest party is Ohm on Fridays and Saturdays, which, although ostensibly gay, attracts a mixed crowd. Ohm was once legendary, but has gone off the boil in recent years. Even so, it still has no serious competition. *Plaza del Callao 4.* ☎ *91-531-01-32. www.ohmclub.es. Cover 10€–15€ includes drink. Metro: Callao. Map p 115.*

Wine Bars

★ **Aloque** CENTRAL MADRID This tiny bar has a big reputation for its incredible selection of wines: There are more than 1,000 on the list. Unusually, it also offers a good choice by the glass (these change regularly). Wine-tasting events and courses are also arranged. The tapas and *raciones* are excellent, and prices are extremely reasonable, so get here early to grab a table. *C/ Torrecilla del Leal 20.* ☎ *91-528-36-62. Metro: Lavapiés or Antón Martín. Map p 115.*

★ **Le Petit Bar** CENTRAL MADRID As small as the name suggests, this red-painted bar offers an interesting selection of wines—including, unusually, a short selection of international wines (one of the owners is French), accompanied by modern tapas: Daily specials are scrawled on a blackboard. They also run wine tastings. *C/ Fúcar 9.* ☎ *91-156-84-66. www.lepetitbar.es. Metro: Antón Martína. Map p 115.*

For live music venues, see p 126. ●

Madrid Arts & Entertainment

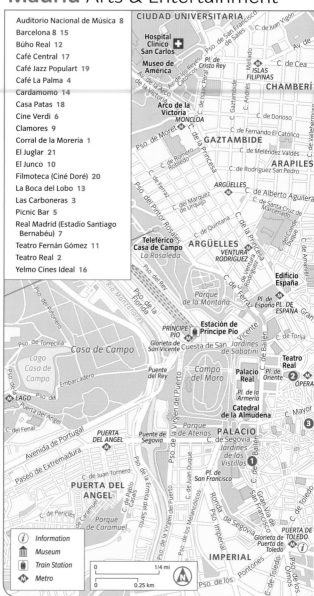

Auditorio Nacional de Música 8
Barcelona 8 15
Búho Real 12
Café Central 17
Café Jazz Populart 19
Café La Palma 4
Cardamomo 14
Casa Patas 18
Cine Verdi 6
Clamores 9
Corral de la Moreria 1
El Juglar 21
El Junco 10
Filmoteca (Ciné Doré) 20
La Boca del Lobo 13
Las Carboneras 3
Picnic Bar 5
Real Madrid (Estadio Santiago Bernabéu) 7
Teatro Fernán Gómez 11
Teatro Real 2
Yelmo Cines Ideal 16

Information
Museum
Train Station
Metro

0   1/4 mi
0   0.25 km

Previous page: Teatro Real.

Arts & Entertainment Best Bets

Best **Concert Acoustics**
★★★ Auditorio Nacional de Música, *C/ Príncipe de Vergara 146* (p 125)

Best **Jazz Club for Romance**
★★ Café Central, *Plaza del Ángel 10* (p 126)

Best **Basement Jazz Dive**
★★ El Junco, *Plaza de Santa Bárbara 10* (p 127)

Best **Flamenco, Flashy Dresses & All**
★★ Casa Patas, *C/ Cañizares 10* (p 126)

Best for **Operatic Glamor**
★★★ Teatro Real, *Plaza Isabel II s/n* (p 127)

Best **Performing Arts Festival**
★★ Los Veranos de la Villa (p 127)

Best **Sporting Event**
★★ Real Madrid, *Estadio Santiago Bernabéu, Paseo de la Castellana* (p 128)

Best for **Theater Performances**
★ Teatro Fernán Gómez, *Plaza de Colón* (p 128)

Best **Original Live Music Venue**
★ El Juglar, *C/ Lavapiés 37* (p 127)

Best for **Up-and-Coming Artists**
Barcelona 8, *C/ Barcelona 8* (p 127)

Best for **Informal Flamenco**
★ Cardamomo, *C/ Echegaray 15* (p 125)

Best **Arthouse Cinema**
★★★ Filmoteca (Ciné Doré), *C/ Santa Isabel 3* (p 125)

Best **Moviehouse for Subtitles**
★★ Cine Verdi, *C/ Bravo Murillo 28* (p 125)

Best for **Free Live Music**
★ Picnic Bar, *Minas 1* (p 128)

Best **All-in-One Venue**
Café La Palma, *C/ La Palma 62* (p 127)

Best **Alternative Rock Festival**
Festimad (p 127)

Teatro Real for operatic glamor.

Arts & Entertainment **A to Z**

Classical Music

★★★ Auditorio Nacional de Música

OUTSKIRTS Madrid's main classical music venue is awkwardly located on the outskirts of the city. It is home to the National Orchestra of Spain and is the first port of call of all major touring orchestras. As well as classical music, it showcases jazz, tango, flamenco, world music, and virtually every other genre imaginable. *C/ Príncipe de Vergara 146.* ☎ *91-337-01-40. www.auditorionacional.mcu. es. Tickets 8€–45€. Metro: Cruz del Rayo or Prosperidad. Map p 123.*

Film

★★ Cine Verdi

NORTH MADRID This arthouse cinema shows a good mix of the cream of Hollywood, offbeat classics, and world cinema. All are shown undubbed and with Spanish subtitles. *C/ Bravo Murillo 28.* ☎ *91-447-39-30. www.cines-verdi.com. Tickets 7.50€, 5€ Mon. Metro: Canal. Map p 123.*

★★★ Filmoteca (Ciné Doré)

CENTRAL MADRID This is a big favorite of mine. Spain's national movie theater is housed in its oldest cinema, the Art Nouveau-style Ciné Doré (built 1922), and features cult classics, actor and director retrospectives, and special seasons. There's a great cafe and bookstore too. *C/ Santa Isabel 3.* ☎ *91-369-11-25. www.mcu.es/cine. Tickets 2.50€. Metro: Antón Martín. Map p 123.*

Yelmo Cines Ideal

CENTRAL MADRID The most central of the multiplexes, with nine screens showing undubbed blockbusters and other movies in *V.O. (versión original)* with Spanish subtitles. *C/ Dr Cortezo 36.* ☎ *91-369-25-18. www.yelmocines.es. Tickets 8€,*

Art Nouveau–styled Ciné Doré.

6.50€ Mon. Metro: Tirso de Molina. Map p 123.

Travel Tip

Most Madrid cinemas have a *día espectador,* usually Monday, when tickets are cheaper.

Flamenco

★ Cardamomo

CENTRAL MADRID   Young locals and foreigners in pursuit of *duende* (soul) flock to this small flamenco bar, where shows take place on the tiny stage nightly from Tuesday to Friday. *C/ Echegaray 15.* ☎ *91-369-07-57. www.cardamomo.net. Tickets from 28€, including drink. Metro: Sevilla or Sol. Map p 123.*

Travel Tip

Our recommended flamenco *tablaos* (shows) offer performances with drinks only or with dinner. The food is often mediocre but dining usually entitles you to better seats.

★★ **Casa Patas** CENTRAL MADRID   An old friend, a prestigious dancer with a long career, recommends this flamenco show above any other in the city. There is a restaurant attached, but the shows are performed in a separate, intimate room where you can feel the sweat of the whirling dancers. *C/ Cañizares 10.* ☎ *91-369-04-96. Tickets from 32€, including drink. Metro: Antón Martin or Tirso de Molina. Map p 123.*

Corral de la Morería CENTRAL MADRID   This is one of the oldest *tablaos* in Madrid, and still attracts some of the finest performers in the flamenco world. *C/ Morería 17.* ☎ *91-365-84-46. www.corraldela moreria.com. Tickets from 36€, including drink. Metro: Ópera or Sol. Map p 122.*

★ **Las Carboneras** CENTRAL MADRID   This popular *tablao* offers dinner and/or drinks with a flamenco show. The food is ordinary, but the shows, performed by top artists, are enthralling. Shows are at 10:30pm on Monday and Thursday through Saturday, with additional shows at 8:30pm Friday and Saturday. *Plaza Conde de Miranda 1.* ☎ *91-542-86-77. www.tablaolas carboneras.com. Dinner and show 58€–68€; drink and show 30€. Metro: Ópera. Map p 122.*

Jazz, Funk & Blues
★★ **Café Central** CENTRAL MADRID   I love this romantic, dimly lit jazz bar, which occupies a beautiful turn-of-the-20th-century former mirror shop, full of gleaming wood and burnished glass. Get here early to bag a table. *Plaza del Ángel 10.* ☎ *91-369-41-43. www.cafecentral madrid.com. Cover 9€–12€. Metro: Sevilla or Sol. Map p 123.*

★ **Café Jazz Populart** CENTRAL MADRID   It's always a squeeze at this classic jazz club in the buzzy Santa Ana district, which attracts a young, bohemian crowd. There are usually two shows a night, and the performers come from around the world. *C/ Huertas 22.* ☎ *91-429-84-07. www.populart.es. No cover. Metro: Antón Martin. Map p 123.*

★ **Clamores** CENTRAL MADRID   This small and much-loved basement jazz venue stages all kinds of concerts, including pop,

Advance Tickets & Listings

For the latest concert, theater, and event listings, pick up a copy of the weekly *Guía del Ocio*, available at newsstands. The Friday edition of the *El Mundo* newspaper comes with an excellent free listings guide, *Metrópoli*. You can also try *In Madrid*, a free English-language magazine found in cafes and bars, or look at www. tbsmagazine.com.

Advance tickets can be purchased at **El Corté Inglés** (p 79) and at **FNAC** (p 77). Other ticket vendors include **Tel-Entrada** (☎ 90-210-12-12; www.telentrada.com), **ServiCaixa** (☎ 90-233-22-11; www.servicaixa.com), and **Tick Tack Ticket** (☎ 90-215-00-25; www. ticktackticket.com). The website www.atrapalo.com is the best for finding discounted tickets.

Madrid's Music Festivals

Madrid hosts several popular music festivals throughout the summer. **Los Veranos de la Villa** (information at www.esmadrid. es) is one of the most prestigious, an eclectic summer-long festival of music, theater, circus, dance, and more. **Sonisphere** (www. sonispherefestivals.com) is a 1-day summer festival in July featuring top international heavy-metal acts. **Festimad** in April/May offers 48 hours of non-stop alternative music from the likes of The Gift and Black Lips (www.festimad.es).

rock, and world music, but its roots are firmly set in jazz and blues. *C/ Alburquerque 14.* ☎ *91-445-79-38. www.salaclamores.com. Cover varies, usually around 6€–12€, sometimes free. Metro: Bilbao. Map p 123.*

★★ El Junco CENTRAL MADRID This has all the right ingredients for a musical dive, with low red lights, exposed brick walls, and huge black-and-white murals. Expect anything from jazz and blues to soul, world music, and pop. *Plaza de Santa Bárbara 10.* ☎ *91-319-20-81. www.eljunco.com. Cover 9€–12€. Metro: Alonso Martínez. Map p 123.*

Opera & Ballet
★★★ Teatro Real CENTRAL MADRID Madrid's opulent opera house is considered one of the finest in the world. It opened in 1850 and is a heady whirl of marble and gilt. A performance here is an unforgettable event—and surprisingly affordable in comparison with other opera houses in Europe. This is also the city's main venue for classical ballet, and seat of the **Orquesta Sinfónica de Madrid** (Madrid Symphony Orchestra). *Plaza Isabel II s/n.* ☎ *91-516-06-60. Tickets 7.60€– 262€. www.teatro-real.com. Metro: Ópera. Map p 122.*

Pop & Rock
Barcelona 8 CENTRAL MADRID A good time is guaranteed at this appealing little venue, which always features interesting artists. Expect anything from indie to local singer-musicians. *C/ Barcelona 8.* ☎ *91-522-96-18. Tickets up to 10€. Metro: Sol. Map p 123.*

Búho Real CENTRAL MADRID This is a cozy little venue, with low-lit corners and wooden beams, which focuses on acoustic music (mainly pop and indie bands). *C/ Regueros 5.* ☎ *91-308-48-51. www.buhoreal.com. Tickets 8€–11€. Metro: Alonso Martínez. Map p 123.*

Café La Palma CENTRAL MADRID This labyrinthine student favorite is a cafe, bar, exhibition space, and live music venue in one. Early in the evening, it is mellow and great for a quiet drink, but things hot up as the evening progresses. *C/ La Palma 62.* ☎ *91-522-50-31. Tickets (concerts only) 6€. Metro: Noviciado. Map p 123.*

★ El Juglar CENTRAL MADRID This is a great, multifunctional space in the heart of multicultural Lavapiés, with a relaxed bar, live gigs by local artists (pop, rock, and a weekly flamenco night), and DJ sessions. *C/ Lavapiés 37.*

Estadio Santiago Bernabéu.

☎ *91-528-43-81. www.salajuglar. com. Tickets usually 5€. Metro: La Latina. Map p 123.*

La Boca del Lobo CENTRAL MADRID   On busy, buzzy, bar-lined Calle Echegaray, this stands out for its original and wide-ranging program of events, including DJ sessions, film screenings, art exhibitions, and book signings. Live gigs could be anything from rock to cabaret. *C/ Echegaray 11.* ☎ *91-429-70-13. www.labocadellobo.com. Tickets up to 10€. Metro: Sevilla. Map p 123.*

★ **Picnic Bar** CENTRAL MADRID One of my favorites in Malasaña, this hippy-chic cafe-bar has free live music and a friendly crowd. *C/ Minas 1. No phone. www.salajuglar.com. Metro: Noviciado. Map p 123.*

Spectator Sports
★★ **Real Madrid (Estadio Santiago Bernabéu)** CENTRAL MADRID   Madrid's immensely popular soccer team—perennially among the best in Europe—plays at the Santiago Bernabéu stadium. Tickets for matches against archrivals F.C. Barcelona are hard to come by, but you can usually get hold of tickets for other matches. For information on the **Real Madrid Museum,** see p 50, ④. *Estadio Santiago Bernabéu, Paseo de la Castellana.* ☎ *91-398-43-70 or 90-230-17-09. www.realmadrid.es. Tickets from 20€. Metro: Santiago Bernabéu. Map p 123.*

Theater
★ **Teatro Fernán Gómez** CENTRAL MADRID   This multifunctional space has a wide-ranging program including theater and concerts in all musical genres. Drama (in Spanish) predominates, however. *Plaza de Colón.* ☎ *91-575-60-80. Tickets 18€–60€. Metro: Cruz del Rayo or Prosperidad. Map p 123.* ●

Lodging **Best Bets**

Best for **Afternoons in the Park**
★★ AC Palacio del Retiro
C/ Alfonso XII 14 (p 134)

Best for **Would-Be Aristocrats**
★★★ Ritz *Plaza de la Lealtad 5 (p 143)*

Best **Business Hotel**
Hesperia Madrid *Paseo de la Castellana 57 (p 136)*

Best for **Cinephiles**
★★ Dormirdcine *C/ Príncipe de Vergara 87 (p 135)*

Best for **Cutting-Edge Design**
★★★ Hotel Silken Puerta de América *Av. de América 41 (p 140)*

Best for **Fashionistas**
★★ Hotel Urban *Carrera de San Jerónimo 34 (p 141)*

Best for **Celeb-Spotting**
★★ Me Madrid *Plaza de Santa Ana 14 (p 141)*

Best **Old-City Location**
★★ Hotel Plaza Mayor *C/ Atocha 3 (p 140)*

Best for **Shopaholics**
★★ Único *Claudio Coello 67 (p 143)*

Best for **Spa Treatments**
★ Radisson Blu Madrid Prado *C/ Moratín 52 (p 143)*

Best for **Light Sleepers**
★ Hospes Madrid *Plaza de la Independencia 3 (p 137)*

Best **Affordable Design**
★ Room Mate Alicia *C/ Prado 2 (p 143)*

Best for **City Views**
★★★ De Las Letras *Gran Vía 11 (p 135)* and ★ Vincci SoMa *C/ Goya 79 (p 144)*

Best for **Families**
★★ AC Palacio del Retiro
C/ Alfonso XII 14 (p 134)

Best **Rooftop Pool**
★ Hotel Emperador *Gran Vía 53 (p 139)*

Best **Family-Run Hostel**
★ Hostal Barrera *C/ Atocha 96 (p 138)*

Best **Luxury Hideaway**
★★★ Casa de Madrid *C/ Arrieta 2 (p 134)*

Most **Palatial Hotel**
★★ Westin Palace *Plaza de las Cortes 7 (p 144)*

Best **Home-Cooked Breakfasts**
★ Abracadabra B&B *C/ Bailen 39 (p 134)*

Best for **Classical Antiquities**
★ Villa Real *Plaza de las Cortes 10 (p 144)*

Best **Airport Hotel**
Clement Barajas *Av. General 43 (p 135)*

Room Mate Alicia.

Previous page: The Westin Palace.

Old Madrid Lodging

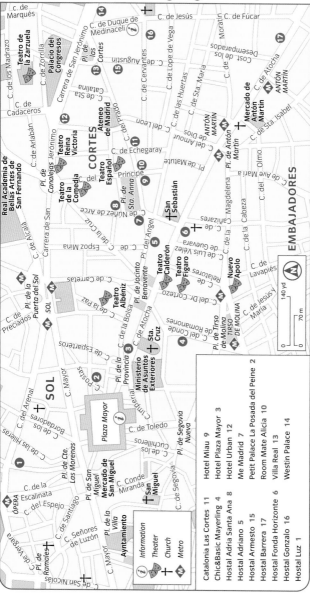

Catalonia Las Cortes 11
Chic&Basic Mayerling 4
Hostal Adria Santa Ana 8
Hostal Adriano 5
Hostal Armesto 15
Hostal Barrera 17
Hostal Fonda Horizonte 6
Hostal Gonzalo 16
Hostal Luz 1

Hotel Miau 9
Hotel Plaza Mayor 3
Hotel Urban 12
Me Madrid 7
Petit Palace La Posada del Peine 2
Room Mate Alicia 10
Villa Real 13
Westin Palace 14

Central Madrid Lodging

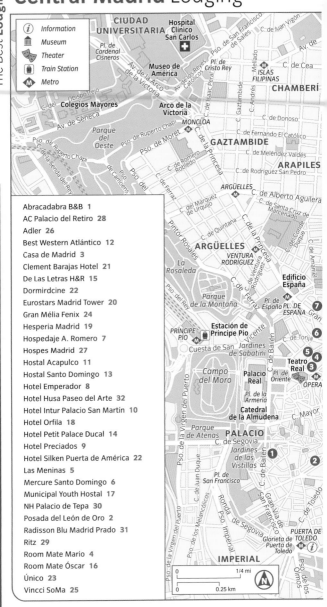

ⓘ	Information
🏛	Museum
🎭	Theater
🚉	Train Station
Ⓜ	Metro

Abracadabra B&B 1
AC Palacio del Retiro 28
Adler 26
Best Western Atlántico 12
Casa de Madrid 3
Clement Barajas Hotel 21
De Las Letras H&R 15
Dormirdcine 22
Eurostars Madrid Tower 20
Gran Mélia Fenix 24
Hesperia Madrid 19
Hospedaje A. Romero 7
Hospes Madrid 27
Hostal Acapulco 11
Hostal Santo Domingo 13
Hotel Emperador 8
Hotel Husa Paseo del Arte 32
Hotel Intur Palacio San Martín 10
Hotel Orfila 18
Hotel Petit Palace Ducal 14
Hotel Preciados 9
Hotel Silken Puerta de América 22
Las Meninas 5
Mercure Santo Domingo 6
Municipal Youth Hostal 17
NH Palacio de Tepa 30
Posada del León de Oro 2
Radisson Blu Madrid Prado 31
Ritz 29
Room Mate Mario 4
Room Mate Óscar 16
Único 23
Vincci SoMa 25

Madrid Lodging **A to Z**

★ **Abracadabra B&B** CENTRAL MADRID A charming couple run this cozy bed-and-breakfast, which offers warmly decorated bedrooms with pretty prints and eclectic artworks. A home-cooked breakfast eaten at the table with your fellow guests kickstarts the day nicely, and it's very handy for the Royal Palace and the old city. Street noise can be a problem. *C/ Bailen 39.* ☎ *65-685-97-84. www.abracadabrabandb. com. 7 units. Doubles 52€–75€. MC, V. Metro: Latina. Map p 132.*

★★ kids **AC Palacio del Retiro** CENTRAL MADRID The former owners of this elegant early-20th-century palace used to exercise their horses on the roof. It's now a sleek, contemporary hotel, and luxurious amenities include a spa and smart restaurant. There's a babysitting service (with prior notice), and parents will be grateful for the Retiro's play areas. *C/ Alfonso XII 14.* ☎ *91-523-74-60. www.ac-hoteles.com. 50 units. Doubles 210€–295€. AE, DC, MC, V. Metro: Retiro. Map p 133.*

Adler CENTRAL MADRID If stark minimalism is not for you, consider this classically elegant hotel in smart Salamanca. The finest shopping is on the doorstep, and the historic center is a short Metro journey away. As with most Madrid hotels, the expensive buffet breakfast is best swapped for a fresh coffee and pastry at a nearby cafe. *C/ Velázquez 14.* ☎ *91-426-32-20. www.adlermadrid.com. 45 units. Doubles 250€–395€. AE, DC, MC, V. Metro: Velázquez. Map p 133.*

Best Western Atlántico CENTRAL MADRID A frothy 19th-century building in the heart of the Gran Vía, this has comfortable, if blandly decorated, bedrooms, which are well soundproofed against street noise. It is worth paying a little more for a balcony. There are inspiring views from the rooftop terrace, and a cheap shuttle bus service to the airport. *Gran Vía 38.* ☎ *91-522-64-80. www. bestwesternhotelatlantico.com. 109 units. Doubles 158€–200€. AE, DC, MC, V. Metro: Gran Vía. Map p 133.*

★★★ **Casa de Madrid** CENTRAL MADRID Imagine staying with an aristocratic cousin in an 18th-century apartment filled with antiques and

Roman Lounge, Casa de Madrid.

Clement Barajas Hotel.

oil paintings, and you have an idea what this exclusive B&B feels like. Breakfast is served on silver trays, and drinks are provided from an honesty bar. Consider using the chauffeur service from the airport. *C/ Arrieta 2.* ☎ *91-559-57-91. www. casademadrid.com. 7 units. Doubles 150€–399€ w/breakfast. DC, MC, V. Metro: Ópera. Map p 132.*

kids Catalonia Las Cortes CEN-TRAL MADRID   An 18th-century *palacete* has been refurbished to contain this central hotel. The suites still contain original frescoes, but the remaining rooms, though comfortable, are rather anonymous. Take a look at the different rooms, if you can, before making a choice. Triple rooms are available, as are babysitting services (on request). *C/ Prado 6* ☎ *91-389-60-51. www. hoteles-catalonia.com. 65 units. Doubles 99€–245€. AE, DC, MC, V. Metro: Sevilla. Map p 131.*

★ **Chic&Basic Mayerling** CEN-TRAL MADRID   Part of a mini-chain, this offers simply but brightly furnished rooms in a former textile factory. Industrial design meets contemporary chic in the bedrooms, which, although on the small side, all have air-conditioning and plasma TVs. Help yourself to a basic buffet breakfast in the designer lobby. *C/ Conde de Ramanones 6.* ☎ *91-420-15-80. www.chicandbasic.com.*

22 units. Doubles 95€–105€. MC, V. Metro: Tirso de Molina. Map p 131.

Clement Barajas Hotel BARAJAS A great choice if you have an early or a late flight, this modern hotel offers cream and beige bedrooms with well-stocked bathrooms, which even have dressing gowns and slippers. There's a regular 24-hour airport shuttle (hourly, 5-min journey), and the free Wi-Fi and minibar are nice touches. *Av. General 43.* ☎ *91-746-03-30. www.clement hoteles.com. 72 units. Doubles 117€–250€. AE, DC, MC, V. Metro: Barajas, then shuttle. Map p 133.*

★★★ **De Las Letras Hotel & Restaurant** CENTRAL MADRID A striking building from 1917, this chic hotel has preserved original details such as the lavish tiles and combined them with modern design. Each room is dedicated to a different writer, with quotations inscribed on the walls. I especially love the suites in the cupolas. The roof terrace bar has knockout views. *Gran Vía 11.* ☎ *91-523-79-80. www.hotel delasletras.com. 108 units. Doubles 125€–280€. AE, DC, MC, V. Metro: Sevilla or Gran Vía. Map p 133.*

★★ **kids Dormirdcine** CENTRAL MADRID   At the quirkiest hotel in town, each room is dedicated to a different director or cult classic. Murals of Charlie Chaplin, the Marx

Hospes Madrid.

Brothers, and King Kong dominate the lobby, while "cooltural" bedrooms feature everyone from Steve McQueen to the Pink Panther. Although not bang in the center, it's well connected by Metro, train, and bus. *C/ Príncipe de Vergara 87.* ☎ *91-411-08-09. www.dormirdcine. com. 85 units. Doubles 90€–150€. MC, V. Metro: Avenida de América. Map p 133.*

Eurostars Madrid Tower CASTELLANA   In the new Cuatro Torres business district, this luxurious hotel occupies 31 floors of one of Spain's tallest skyscrapers. The contemporary rooms are spacious and offer superlative skyline views, and are complemented by superb facilities including a spa and panoramic restaurant. The old center is a quick Metro ride away. *Paseo de la Castellana.* ☎ *91-334-27-00. www. eurostarsmadridtower.com. 474 units. Doubles 135€–200€. AE, DC, MC, V. Metro: Begoña. Map p 133.*

Gran Mélia Fenix SALAMANCA This plush hotel has catered to a long list of celebrity guests, from the Beatles to the Beckhams. The grand neoclassical building contains classically decorated and lavish guest rooms and salons, as well as an upscale restaurant and cocktail bar. Go for broke on the Royal Service premium suites, which have private butlers. *C/ Hermosilla 2, Plaza de Colón.* ☎ *91-431-67-00. www. gran-melia-fenix.com. 215 units. Doubles 220€–390€. AE, DC, MC, V. Metro: Colón. Map p 133.*

Hesperia Madrid CENTRAL MADRID   A modern, sophisticated hotel, this is located in the business district in northern Madrid. Rooms were decorated by Pascua Ortega and bathrooms are filled with Bulgari toiletries. The rooftop Sky Gym offers state-of-the-art equipment and staggering city views; the Santceloni restaurant is superb (p 109). *Paseo Castellana 57.* ☎ *91-210-80-00. www.hesperia.com. 170 units. Doubles 129€–250€. AE, DC, MC, V. Metro: Gregorio Marañón. Map p 133.*

★ **Hospedaje A. Romero** CENTRAL MADRID   Run by a friendly mother-and-son team, this is located upstairs in a classic Madrileño building complete with charming antique lift. The rooms are basic, and the bathrooms tiny, but everything is kept spotless. Free Wi-Fi is available, and guests have free use of the computer terminal in the lobby. *Gran Vía 64.* ☎ *91-559-76-61. www. hospedajeromero.com. 8 units. Doubles 50€–60€. MC, V. Metro: Plaza de España. Map p 132.*

★ **Hospes Madrid** CENTRAL MADRID A pleasing fusion of classical architecture and chic interior design, this sits next to the Retiro. Rooms are among the quietest in the city, and are beautifully furnished with impressive bathrooms. Top-floor duplex suites are especially luxurious. There's a spa, a chillout zone on the patio, and a good restaurant. *Plaza de la Independencia 3.* ☎ *91-432-29-11. www. hospes.es. 41 units. Doubles 150€– 280€. AE, DC, MC, V. Metro: Retiro. Map p 133.*

kids **Hostal Acapulco** CENTRAL MADRID Affordable, friendly, and central, the Hostal Acapulco has few frills but plenty of old-fashioned charm. An antique lift propels you upstairs, where chintz prints await. There are triple and quadruple rooms, which are good for families. It's centrally located, with most of the main sights within walking distance. *C/ Salud 13, Plaza del Carmen.* ☎ *91-531-19-45. www.hostal acapulco.com. 16 units. Doubles 55€–90€. MC, V. Metro: Gran Vía. Map p 133.*

★ **kids** **Hostal Adria Santa Ana** CENTRAL MADRID Run by the same delightful owners as the Hostal Adriano (*see above*), this is a tad more luxurious and slightly pricier than its older sister. Each room is individually decorated in a different color scheme and style, and all have ensuite bathrooms, air-conditioning, and free Wi-Fi. Triples and quadruples are available. *C/ de la Cruz 26.*

☎ *91-521-13-39. www.hostal adriano.com. 10 units. Doubles 60€– 110€. MC, V. Metro: Sol. Map p 131.*

★ **kids** **Hostal Adriano** CENTRAL MADRID Bright, individual rooms, a great location near the Puerta del Sol in the heart of the city, plus rock-bottom prices make this a winner. Guest rooms are small, and bathrooms tiny, but all have air-conditioning, satellite TV, and free Wi-Fi. Some can be adapted (just) for four, making them suitable for budget-minded families. *C/ de la Cruz 26.* ☎ *91-521-13-39. www. hostal adriano.com. 15 units. Doubles 55€– 95€. MC, V. Metro: Sol. Map p 131.*

★ **Hostal Armesto** CENTRAL MADRID The Prado, as well as the restaurants and nightlife of Santa Ana, are on the doorstep of this comfortable hostal. Bedrooms are modestly but attractively decorated with print bedspreads and draped curtains, and all have air-conditioning and ensuite bathrooms. Triples are available. Great value. *C/ San Agustín 6.* ☎ *91-429-90-31. www. hostalarmesto.com. 8 units. Doubles 35€–70€. MC, V. Metro: Sol or Sevilla. Map p 131.*

Hostal Acapulco.

Hostal Barrera.

★ **Hostal Barrera** CENTRAL MADRID The immaculate little rooms, all with heating and air-conditioning, are perfectly adequate at this family-run *hostal*, but the real draw is the helpful staff. Nothing is too much trouble, and they will even decorate your map with the best places to see and to eat and drink at. The only drawback is street noise, so pack earplugs. *C/ Atocha 96.* ☎ *91-527-53-81. www.hostal barrera.com. 14 units. Doubles 45€– 90€. AE, MC, V. Metro: Antón Martín. Map p 131.*

Hostal Fonda Horizonte CENTRAL MADRID A small, family-run *hostal*,

Hostal Fonda Horizonte.

with an enthusiastic and multilingual young manager, this offers a handful of eccentric, occasionally flamboyant rooms. The prettiest have flower-decked balconies overlooking the street. Not all boast ensuite bathrooms, and street noise can be a problem. *C/ Atocha 28.* ☎ *91-369-09-96. www.hostalhorizonte.com. 65 units. Doubles 35€–85€. Metro: Antón Martín. Map p 131.*

Hostal Gonzalo CENTRAL MADRID A modest *hostal* tucked away in the quieter reaches of buzzy Santa Ana, this features functional but immaculately kept rooms (all with ensuite bathrooms) in a renovated 19th-century townhouse. A stone's throw from the three big museums, and with scores of restaurants and bars on the doorstep, it couldn't be better located. *C/ Cervantes 34.* ☎ *91-429-27-14. www.hostalgonzalo.com. 14 units. Doubles 50€–75€. MC, V. Metro: Antón Martín. Map p 131.*

★ **Hostal Luz** CENTRAL MADRID Renovated in 2010, the bedrooms at this charming *hostal* are traditionally decorated with floral curtains and bedspreads in shades of pink and peach. Choose from rooms with ensuite facilities, or with shared bathrooms for a bit less. A simple breakfast is included, there's free

Wi-Fi, and it's bang in the center. *C/ de las Fuentes 10.* ☎ *91-542-07-59. www.hostalluz.com. 20 units. Doubles 59€–100€ w/breakfast. Metro: Ópera. Map p 131.*

★ Hostal Santo Domingo

CENTRAL MADRID   After a thorough overhaul in 2007, this long-established *hostal* has emerged with a new 21st-century look. The rooms are compact but cheerfully decorated in bright, modern prints, prettily offset by original tiling and wrought-iron balconies. The bathrooms feature rainfall showers and some even have Jacuzzis. *C/ Luna 6.* ☎ *91-531-32-90. www.hostalsantodomingo.es. 20 units. Doubles 69€–120€. AE, MC, V. Metro: Callao. Map p 133.*

★ kids Hotel Emperador

CENTRAL MADRID   This large, modern hotel caters for business travelers, which can mean great bargains at weekends. Rooms are smallish and decked out in anonymous chain-hotel style, but its best feature is the rooftop pool (open May–Sept), one of very few in the city, and the perfect place for a dip after a long day. *Gran Vía 53.* ☎ *91-547-28-00. www. emperadorhotel.com. 241 units. Doubles 85€–160€. MC, V. Metro: Santo Domingo. Map p 133.*

Roof-top pool at Hotel Emperador.

Hotel Husa Paseo del Arte

CENTRAL MADRID   Art fans will love this smart hotel, around the corner from the Reina Sofía and just a 5-minute walk from the Thyssen and the Prado. It was built in 2006, and rooms feature streamlined furnishings and neutral colors; some have floor-to-ceiling windows with breathtaking views. Internet deals can bring prices very low. *C/ Atocha 123.* ☎ *91-298-48-00. www.hotel husapaseodelarte.com. 260 units. Doubles 90€–180€. AE, DC, MC, V. Metro: Atocha. Map p 133.*

★ Hotel Intur Palacio San Martín

CENTRAL MADRID   A 19th-century *palacete* near the Plaza Mayor, this has retained its original lift and staircase. Traditional wooden furnishings provide a nice change from the stark minimalism favored by many Madrid hotels, and the prints and draped curtains add a cozy feel. There's a decent restaurant with rooftop views, and free Wi-Fi. *Plaza de San Martín 5.* ☎ *91-701-50-00. www.hotelpalaciosanmartin.es. 94 units. Doubles 120€–220€. AE, DC, MC, V. Metro: Opera. Map p 133.*

Hotel Miau

CENTRAL MADRID   The Miau is nicely located overlooking lively Plaza de Santa Ana. Plainly

furnished rooms are brightened with modern art. Interior rooms, without views, are quieter, but the best are those overlooking the colorful babble of the plaza. Breakfast is basic. *C/ Principe 26.* ☎ *91-369-71-20. www.hotelmiau.com. 75 units. Doubles 195€–315€ w/breakfast. AE, DC, MC, V. Metro: Sol. Map p 131.*

★ **Hotel Orfila** CENTRAL MADRID For old-world charm, you won't do better than this graceful hotel in a 19th-century mansion. Rooms and suites are individually decorated with antiques, and the service is outstanding. The excellent restaurant and tearoom look out over a luxuriant secret garden, and provide an oasis of peace at the end of a long day. *C/ Orfila 6.* ☎ *91-702-77-70. www.hotelorfila.com. 32 units. Doubles 200€–350€. AE, DC, MC, V. Metro: Alsonso Martinez. Map p 133.*

Hotel Petit Palace Ducal CENTRAL MADRID At this converted 19th-century townhouse just off the Gran Vía, bedrooms are small but smartly finished with cream-colored bed linen, dark wooden furnishings, and 21st-century amenities including Wi-Fi. Go for the rooms on the

Hotel Miau.

upper floors, which are slightly quieter. Standard rates are high but Internet deals can make it affordable. *C/ Hortaleza 3.* ☎ *91-421-10-43. www.hthoteles.com. 60 units. Doubles 90€–340€. AE, DC, MC, V. Metro: Gran Vía. Map p 133.*

★★ **Hotel Plaza Mayor** CENTRAL MADRID The location of this family-run hotel, around the corner from Plaza Mayor, can't be bettered. One step from the door and you are in the historic heart of Habsburg Madrid. Rooms are bright and welcoming, and the Palomar suite, a sunny attic with its own tiny terrace, is well worth the small extra cost. Book well ahead. *C/ Atocha 3.* ☎ *91-360-06-06. www.h-plaza mayor.com. 34 units. Doubles 70€–140€. MC, V. Metro: Sol. Map p 131.*

★ kids **Hotel Preciados** CENTRAL MADRID This modern hotel is located on the main shopping street, with all the major city attractions nearby. Bedrooms are typical of chain hotels, bland but well equipped. Best of all, this is one place where street noise rarely penetrates. Extras include free minibar and free Wi-Fi. Suites are good value if traveling with children. *C/ Preciados 37.* ☎ *91-454-44-00. www.preciados hotel.com. 73 units. Doubles 140€–300€. AE, DC, MC, V. Metro: Callao. Map p 133.*

★★★ **Hotel Silken Puerta de América** CENTRAL MADRID This isn't just a hotel, it's an experience. A different, world-renowned architect has designed each floor in homage to contemporary design: Crazy colors by Javier Mariscal, Zen-like peace by Isozaki, and (my favorite) surreal white sculptural surrounds by Zaha Hadid. It is a 10-minute taxi-ride or Metro from the center. *Av. de América 41.* ☎ *91-744-54-00. www.hoteles-silken.com. 342 units. Doubles 140€–450€. AE, DC, MC, V.*

Hotel Silken Puerta de América.

Metro: Cartagena or Avenida de América. Map p 133.

★★ **Hotel Urban** CENTRAL MADRID The coolest hotel in town, this boasts glass and gold decor and luxuries such as a rooftop plunge pool. Bedrooms are small, so consider splashing out on a suite. The glamorous restaurant and rooftop bars are the refuge of the über-hip. It's full of fine art, including a small museum of Egyptian antiquities. *Carrera de San Jerónimo 34.* ☎ *91-787-77-70. www.derbyhotels.com. 102 units. Doubles 215€–475€. AE, DC, MC, V. Metro: Sevilla. Map p 131.*

★★ **kids Las Meninas** CENTRAL MADRID An elegant boutique hotel near the Royal Palace, this has smart rooms furnished in shades of cream, rose, and dove gray. Triple rooms suit families, and guests can use the rooftop gym (free) and sauna (small charge) at their partner hotel, the Ópera, around the corner. *C/ Campomanes 7.* ☎ *91-541-28-05. www.hotelmeninas.com. 37 units. Doubles 90€–130€. MC, V. Metro: Ópera. Map p 132.*

★★ **Me Madrid** CENTRAL MADRID This glamorous hotel occupies a wedding cake of a building constructed in the early 20th century. Inside, dazzling white-and-gold decor is the theme, with models and DJs draped languidly on sofas. Rooms are equipped with iPods and martini bars, and the Level floor boasts the most luxurious suites in Madrid. *Plaza de Santa Ana 14.* ☎ *91-701-60-25. www.memadrid.com. 192 units. Doubles 145€–280€. AE, DC, MC, V. Metro: Sol. Map p 131.*

Mercure Santo Domingo CENTRAL MADRID A handy location just off the Gran Vía, an historic building, and an elegant interior all combine to make this a good, central choice. It's enjoyably

Me Madrid.

Reception, Hotel Urban.

old-fashioned, and the hallways are filled with antique paintings and sculptures. Ideal for senior travelers. *Plaza Santo Domingo 13.* ☎ *91-547-98-00. www.hotelsanto domingo.com. 119 units. Doubles 157€–235€. AE, DC, MC, V. Metro: Santo Domingo. Map p 132.*

Municipal Youth Hostal CEN-

TRAL MADRID   The city-run youth hostel provides clean, functional accommodations in dorm rooms for four to six people. Decorated in black, white, and red, it offers extras such as microwave ovens, laundry, pool table, and TV room. Don't come looking to party at the hostel itself; however, you can take their fun tours. *C/ Mejía Lequerica 21.* ☎ *91-593-96-88. www.ajmadrid.es. 122 beds. Beds 19€–25€ per person. AE, MC, V. Metro: Alonso Martínez. Map p 133.*

★ NH Palacio de Tepa CENTRAL

MADRID   The former residence of the Counts of Montijo and Tepa has been transformed into one of the smartest hotels in Santa Ana. Rooms are decorated in a palette of muted creams, browns, and greens, and some boast wooden floors and vaulted ceilings. There's a small gym, a good restaurant, and a superb tapas bar (Estado Puro).

C/ San Sebastián 2. ☎ *91-330-24-00. www.nh-hotels.com. 85 units. Doubles 19€–209€. AE, DC, MC, V. Metro: Antón Martín. Map p 133.*

Petit Palace La Posada del

Peine CENTRAL MADRID   Occupying the building that once contained the oldest inn in Madrid, this sits on a cobbled street by Plaza Mayor. It has been revamped to house a modest, modern hotel, with chic, if rather small, rooms, and a smattering of original details to add coziness. All the main sights are a short stroll away. *C/ Postas 17.* ☎ *91-523-81-51. www.hthoteles.com. 75 units. Doubles 160€–250€. AE, DC, MC, V. Metro: Sol. Map p 131.*

★ Posada del León de Oro

CENTRAL MADRID   Slap bang in the middle of lively La Latina, this is a contemporary hotel slotted into an historic building. Bedrooms are furnished with sleek minimalism and splashes of bold color (go for the ones with a terrace and try to avoid those on the lower floors). There's an excellent restaurant and wine bar downstairs. *C/ Cava Baja 12.* ☎ *91-119-14-94. www.posadadel leondeoro.com. 17 units. Doubles 150€–270€. AE, DC, MC, V. Metro: La Latina. Map p 132.*

★ Radisson Blu Madrid Prado

CENTRAL MADRID   This global chain chose to go (relatively) small with its first hotel in Madrid. A 19th-century mansion opposite the Prado has become a chic urban bolt-hole, with a huge, dedicated staff. Contemporary bedrooms feature pared-down Scandinavian-style design, softened with plush fabrics, and there's a spa with a small pool. *C/ Moratín 52.* ☎ *91-524-26-26. www.radissonblu.com. 54 units. Doubles 185€–415€. AE, DC, MC, V. Metro: Antón Martín. Map p 133.*

The Ritz.

★★★ Ritz

CENTRAL MADRID   The grande dame of Madrid hotels is a huge, white Belle Époque confection: Alfonso XIII ordered the original palace's conversion into a hotel, and it remains a favorite with visiting aristocrats (who choose the Royal Suite). Sumptuous decor (no minimalism here) and attentive service make this a very special place to stay. *Plaza de la Lealtad 5.* ☎ *91-420-37-67. www.ritzmadrid.com. 165 units. Doubles 350€–540€. AE, DC, MC, V. Metro: Banco de España. Map p 133.*

★ Room Mate Alicia

CENTRAL MADRID   Part of an innovative, small (but expanding) chain, Alicia offers style on a budget in the atmospheric nightlife zone of Plaza de Santa Ana. A stunning staircase made of steel squiggles leads to the bedrooms, where white predominates. In summer, consider a suite with private terrace, and take a siesta on the sun lounger. *C/ Prado 2.* ☎ *91-389-85-48. www.room-matehotels.com. 37 units. Doubles 110€–200€. AE, DC, MC, V. Metro: Sol. Map p 131.*

★ Room Mate Mario

CENTRAL MADRID   The original Room Mate hotel, and still a big favorite of mine. The street is one of the nicest in the city, an elegant curve lined with

trees. Bold, contemporary decor, compact but well-equipped rooms, and friendly service are the hallmarks of the company. Plus there's free Wi-Fi and a simple buffet breakfast. *C/ Campomanes 4.* ☎ *91-548-85-48. www.room-matehotels.com. 54 units. Doubles 85€–134€ w/ breakfast. AE, DC, MC, V. Metro: Ópera. Map p 132.*

★ Room Mate Óscar

CENTRAL MADRID   Another option from the excellent Room Mate stable, this is the most fashionable of the lot. The rooftop splash pool (access costs 20€ per half-day) hosts poolside DJ sessions, which have become a summer institution, but the noise might keep light sleepers awake. *Plaza Vázquez de Mella 12.* ☎ *91-701-11-73. www.room-matehotels.com. 75 units. Doubles 85€–190€. AE, DC, MC, V. Metro: Chueca. Map p 133.*

★★ Único

SALAMANCA   A favorite with fashionistas, thanks to its location in the chi-chi Salamanca shopping district, this occupies a turn-of-the-20th-century *palacete*. It features a twirling marble staircase, black-and-white bedrooms, the superb Ramon Freixa restaurant, and a patio garden. Personal shoppers and beauty treatments can be arranged. *C/ Claudio Coello 67.*

Apartment Rental

Renting an apartment can be an economical and convenient option, particularly if you are traveling with young children. Useful rental websites include **www.friendlyrentals.com**, **www.go madrid.com**, and **www.mad4rent.com**. Prices usually start at around 100€ per day for a two-bedroom flat in the center, and most apartments require a minimum stay of 2 or 3 days. Prices usually reflect the district: Those in upscale Salamanca are more expensive, while in humble Lavapiés you'll find bargains. There are plenty of grocery stores and fresh-produce markets in the city center.

☎ 91-781-01-73. www.unicohotel madrid.com. 44 units. Doubles 175€–250€. AE, DC, MC, V. Metro: Serrano. Map p 133.

★ **Villa Real** CENTRAL MADRID Refinement and luxury go hand in hand at this elegant *palacete*, a stone's throw from the Prado. Not as cutting-edge as the nearby Hotel Urban (in the same chain), this nonetheless oozes effortless style. The light-filled interiors meld classical elegance with contemporary art and furnishings. Summer rates can be a bargain. *Plaza de las Cortes 10.* ☎ 91-420-37-67.

The Belle Epoque Westin Palace.

www.derbyhoteles.com. 113 units. Doubles 171€–275€. AE, DC, MC, V. Metro: Banco de España. Map p 131.

★★ kids **Vincci SoMa** CENTRAL MADRID   Most rooms here are spacious by Madrid standards, and the suites have wonderful terraces with sun loungers. It is close to the Retiro Gardens and the upscale Salamanca neighborhood. Triples and fully equipped apartments make a good choice for families. *C/ Goya 79.* ☎ 91-435-75-45. www.vinccihoteles.com. 177 units. Doubles 85€–180€. AE, DC, MC, V. Metro: Goya. Map p 133.

★★ kids **Westin Palace** CENTRAL MADRID   This Belle Epoque hotel is a Madrid institution, offering palatial luxury and stellar service. Meticulously renovated, it features sumptuous classic decor complemented by essential 21st-century services. Gym, hairdresser, and even a children's club (the Westin Kids Club) are among the amenities. *Plaza de las Cortes 7.* ☎ 91-360-80-00. www. westinpalacemadrid.com. 467 units. Doubles 290€–375€. MC, V. Metro: Banco de España. Map p 131. ●

Aranjuez

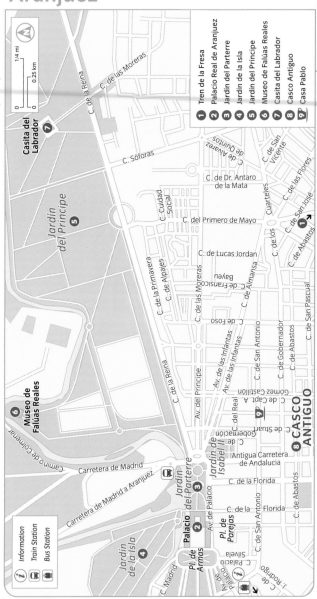

Previous page: Sinagoga del Tránsito.

Aranjuez, beautifully set against the slow curves of the River Tajo, has been a royal retreat for centuries. The Bourbons built the present, lavish 18th-century summer palace on the green riverbanks, amid heavenly, tree-shaded gardens. The delightful town is a tranquil antidote to the energetic capital. START: **Train from Atocha Station (see Practical Matters, below)). Trip length: 1 day.**

① ★★ kids Tren de la Fresa.
Standard trains and buses leave regularly for Aranjuez, but nothing beats the romance of the Tren de la Fresa. In early summer, the "Strawberry Train" puffs its way here, pulling a string of wooden carriages. Aranjuez is famous for its strawberries, and girls in medieval dress hand them out to train passengers. Harry Potter fans will feel like they're on the Hogwarts Express.
🕐 *1 hr. Reservations* ☎ *90-232-03-20. Tickets 26€ adults, 18€ children 4–12, free for 3 and under (includes guided tour of Palacio Real, bus tour, and admission to Royal Barge Museum).Trains usually run weekends from early May to mid-July, but check timetable at www.renfe.com, or at the tourist office.*

Palacio Real de Aranjuez.

② ★★ Palacio Real de Aranjuez. Felipe II commissioned the first permanent royal palace here on the banks of the river in 1561. It was subsequently transformed by the frivolous Spanish Bourbons, who sought to emulate the French court at Versailles. Most of what survived dates to the 18th and 19th centuries, and is as fluffy and ornate as the original palace was restrained and austere. Highlights of the rich interior include the rococo **Porcelain Room,** entirely covered in porcelain chinoiserie, and the **Arabic Cabinet,** which was inspired by the Alhambra in Granada. Anyone interested in royal fashion will be fascinated by the exhibition of wedding gowns worn by the present queen, her daughters, and her popular

Statue and fountain in the garden of the Palacio Real.

daughter-in-law, Leticia. ⏱ *1½ hr. Plaza de Parejas.* ☎ *91-891-03-05. www.patrimonionacional.es. Admission 5€ adults with guided visit, 4.50€ adults non-guided visit, 4€ children 5–16, free for under-5s. Palace plus guided visit to private salons 7€ adults, 5€ children 5–16, free for under-5s. Combined ticket to palace and Royal Barge Museum 8€ adults, 7€ children 5–16, free for under-5s. Oct–Mar daily 10am–5:15pm, Apr–Sept daily 10am–6:15pm.*

❸ ★ Jardín del Parterre. The palace is merely the warm-up to the gardens, which are the real draw of verdant Aranjuez. The formal Parterre gardens gracefully flank the eastern facade of the palace and are laid out in the French style fashionable in the 17th century. ⏱ *20 min. Free admission. Oct–Mar daily 8am–6:30pm, Apr–Sept daily 8am–8:30pm.*

❹ ★ Jardín de la Isla. These charming gardens are surrounded by the slow undulations of the River Tajo and are one of the few survivors of the manor house that once

stood here, and which was used by Ferdinand and Isabella as their summer retreat before the construction of the Royal Palace. ⏱ *20 min. Free admission. Oct–Mar daily 8am–6:30pm, Apr–Sept daily 8am–8:30pm.*

❺ Jardín del Príncipe. This green, tree-shaded oasis is the largest of the royal gardens at Aranjuez, and a sheer delight to explore on foot. It was commissioned by the future Carlos IV, then the Prince of Asturias (hence the name, "the Prince's Garden"), and designed between 1772 and 1804. Huge trees—including oaks, cypresses, and magnolias—are arranged around cool walkways, fountains and statues are dotted in shady bowers, and peacocks strut and shriek. ⏱ *1 hr. Free admission. Oct–Mar daily 8am–6:30pm, Apr–Sept daily 8am–8:30pm.*

❻ Museo de Falúas Reales. Languid royals once drifted along the river in their grand pleasure boats and barges, and these have been gathered together in the fascinating Museo de Falúas (Royal Barge Museum). My favorite is a lovely 17th-century Venetian gondola with gilded nymphs and flowers. ⏲ *45 min. C/ de la Reina, in Jardín del Príncipe.* ☎ *91-891-03-05. Admission 3€ adults, 2€ children 5–16 and seniors, free for under-5s. Combined ticket to palace and Royal Barge Museum 8€ adults, 7€ children 5–16, free for under-5s. Free on Wed for E.U. citizens with photo ID. Apr–Sept Tues–Sun and public hols 10am–6:15pm, Oct–Mar 10am–5:15pm.*

❼ Casita del Labrador. The "Laborer's Cottage" was constructed between 1791 and 1803. Despite the name, it bears no resemblance to a cottage, and its function was entirely related to the pursuit of pleasure. A large, elegant summer pavilion, it is filled with an array of porcelain, statues, paintings, tapestries, clocks, and other works of art, all of which are painstakingly (and somewhat boringly) described on the (obligatory) guided tour. ⏲ *45 min. Plaza de Parejas.* ☎ *91-891-03-05. www.patrimonio nacional.es. Admission 5€ adults, 4€ children 5–16, free for under-5s. Oct–Mar Tues–Sun 10am–5pm, Apr–Sept 10am–6pm.*

❽ ★ Casco Antiguo. The elegant Casco Antiguo (Old Quarter) of Aranjuez is characterized by broad boulevards and expansive squares. Unlike other towns, which grew up organically over the centuries, Aranjuez was carefully planned, then laid out in the 1740s. Numerous royal residences and baroque churches are incorporated into the fine ensemble. ⏲ *45 min.*

❾ Casa Pablo. A lovely old-fashioned tavern established in 1941, this serves classic Castilian cuisine, as well as the sweet strawberries and plump white asparagus for which the town is famous. *C/ Almíbar 42.* ☎ *91-891-14-51. Dishes 14€–19€.*

Practical Matters—Aranjuez

The wonderful Tren de la Fresa (see above, ❶) is the most romantic way to reach Aranjuez, but the service only runs for a few weekends each year in early summer. Regular trains from Madrid's Atocha station (taking 44 min; 4.40€ each way) are the most convenient way to reach the town. Alternatively, a bus service operated by Continental (☎ 90-219-87-88) departs from Madrid's Méndez Álvaro bus station (1 hr; 4.20€). The **Tourist Information Office** is at Antigua Carretera de Andalucía s/n (☎ 91-891-04-27; www.aranjuez.es).

San Lorenzo de El Escorial

1. Bourbon Apartments
2. Pinacoteca & Museo de Arqueologia
3. Habsburg Apartments
4. Panteón de los Reyes
5. Real Basílica
6. Salas Capitulares
7. Biblioteca
8. Casita del Infante & Casita del Príncipe
9. San Lorenzo de El Escorial
10. La Sartén Por El Mango

Rising austerely from the Sierras north of Madrid, the vast Monasterio de San Lorenzo de El Escorial was constructed in the late 16th century for fanatically religious Felipe II (1527–98). Built on a colossal scale, the palace-monastery also included a convent, school, library, and royal pantheon. START: **Train from Atocha Station (see Practical Matters, below). Trip length: 1 day.**

❶ ★★ Bourbon Apartments. The fun-loving Bourbons disliked gloomy El Escorial, but they did their best to brighten up some of the apartments for their own use. Hung with sumptuous tapestries, they are easily the cheeriest section of the palace. Their apartments also contain the **Sala de las Batallas,** a vaulted hall with an enormous fresco depicting great Spanish military victories. ⏲ *30 min.*

❷ ★ Pinacoteca & Museo de Arqueología. Galleries adjoining the Habsburg apartments contain two museums: The **Pinacoteca,** with a fine painting collection (including works by Hieronymus Bosch, who was much liked by Felipe II); and the **Archaeology Museum,** with a fascinating exhibition describing the mechanics of the palace's construction. ⏲ *40 min.*

❸ ★ Habsburg Apartments. Created for Felipe II, the apartments are surprisingly humble and delightfully intimate, with pretty blue-and-white tiles and views over forests and mountains. In these charming rooms, Felipe II and his advisors heard the crushing news of the failure of the Spanish Armada, and of the country's bankruptcy as the king pursued punishing wars against the Protestant Dutch and Muslim Ottomans. Felipe's apartments were built above the Basilica, and his deathbed is still pressed up against

Monasterio de San Lorenzo de El Escorial.

Statue on the monastery wall.

the opening through which he could hear mass being said. 🕐 *30 min.*

④ ★ Panteón de los Reyes.

When Felipe II conceived his new palace-monastery, he sought to find a suitable burial place for his parents, Charles V (Carlos I of Spain) and Isabella of Portugal. The spectacular, marble-and-gold **Pantheon of the Kings** houses 26 marble sepulchers, which contain the remains of almost every Spanish monarch from the 16th century onward. According to an old tradition, queens are only interred here if they are the mother of kings. Queens who didn't bear a king, as well as princes and princesses, are buried in the adjoining, labyrinthine 19th-century **Pantheon of the Princes,** added at the command of Isabel II. In a rather gruesome ritual, the remains of dead monarchs are left in the *pudridero* (Rotting Room) for 50 years before being moved into the Pantheon. The parents of the present king, Juan Carlos I, are in the *pudridero*, awaiting removal to the last empty marble sepulcher. A decision has yet to be made as to where the currently living members

of the Royal Family will be interred after their demise. 🕐 *30 min.*

⑤ ★ Real Basílica.

The Royal Basilica was the very soul of the El Escorial complex. It was designed, like the rest of the palace, by Juan Bautista de Toledo and his pupil Juan de Herrera, clearly influenced by that other great monument to the Counter-Reformation: St. Peter's Basilica in Rome. The soaring dome is all the more impressive for being virtually unadorned, but the high altar is a dazzling swirl of color and gold. There are 43 altars, so that several masses could be said simultaneously. Some contain part of Felipe II's enormous collection of reliquaries, to which the king was very attached. More than 7,500 elaborate coffers, allegedly containing the bones, hair, and nails of various saints, are scattered throughout the complex. 🕐 *30 min.*

⑥ ★ Salas Capitulares (Painting Collection).

The Sacristy and Chapterhouses contain more of El Escorial's vast collection of paintings, gathered beneath frescoed ceilings. The best, however, were creamed off for inclusion in the Pinacoteca (**2**). ⏱ *20 min.*

7 ★ **Biblioteca (Library).** The beautiful library boasts gleaming wood paneling and elaborate frescoes. It was built to house Felipe II's enormous book collection, which numbered more than 40,000 volumes. Ironically, despite Felipe's avid support of the Inquisition that destroyed countless "heretical" works, his library, watched over by Benito Arias Montano, contains priceless Greek, Latin, Hebrew, and Arabic manuscripts that were rescued from the flames. ⏱ *30 min.*

8 ★ **Casita del Infante & Casita del Príncipe.** These two frothy 18th-century pavilions, surrounded by charming gardens, are replete with stucco swirls and frescoes. ⏱ *1 hr.*

9 **San Lorenzo de El Escorial.** The sheer scale of El Escorial is overwhelming, but the relaxed little town of San Lorenzo de El Escorial, with its mountainous backdrop, is a fine place to recover. The *casco histórico* (old quarter) is appealing, with its arcaded streets and charming squares. ⏱ *30 min.*

10 **La Sartén Por El Mango.** On the edge of town, this restaurant may not look special from the outside, but it serves truly delectable, market-fresh cuisine. There's a good-value set lunch menu, and a terrace in summer. *C/ Juan de Toledo 19.* ☎ *91-896-13-13. www.restaurantelasartenporelmango.es. Set lunch 16.50€.*

Practical Matters: El Escorial

Trains (1 hr 5 min; ☎ 90-232-03-20; www.renfe.com) make (at least hourly) departures from Madrid's Atocha station to El Escorial; local buses 661 and 664 connect with the center. By car from Madrid, take the A6 highway (toll) or the M505. The **Tourist Information Office** (☎ 91-890-03-13; www.sanlorenzoturismo.org) is at Calle Grimaldi 4.

El Escorial, Calle Juan de Borbón y Battemberg s/n (☎ 91-890-59-02; www.patrimonionacional.es), is open October to March Tuesday through Sunday 10am to 5pm, April to September Tuesday through Sunday 10am–6pm. Admission costs 10€ adults with a guided visit, 8€ adults for a self-guided visit; 3.50€ to 4€ senior citizens and children aged 5–16; under-5s enter free. Admission to the Basílica only is free.

Guided tours from Madrid usually combine visits to El Escorial with the **Valle de los Caídos (Valley of the Fallen).**

Toledo

Paseo de Canónigos

Glorieta de la Reconquista

Puerta Alfonso VI

0 ___ 1/2 mi
0 ___ 0.50 km

Av. Más del Ribero

Pso. del Circo Romano

Paseo del Cristo de la Vega

Av. del Puente de la Cava

Paseo de Recaredo

Subida de la Granja

Ermita del Cristo de la Vega

Hostel del Cardenal

Santo Domingo el Real
Pl. de la Merced
C. Buzones
C. de la Merced
C. Algibes

Convento Carmelitas Descalzas

Santo Domingo el Antiguo

Puerta del Cambrón
Pl. Santa Teresa de Jesús
C. Sta. Leocadia

Pso. de Recaredo

Pl. San Juan de los Reyes

Palacio de la Cava

Bajada de San Martín

Col. de Doncellas

Pl. de la Virgén de Gracia

C. G. de la Vega
Pl. de Padilla

S. Clemente

Casa de Mesa
C. de San Román

Museo de los Concilios
San Pedro Mártir
C. Alfonso

C...Cava Baja

9 Monasterio de San Juan de los Reyes
C. del Angel

C. las Bulas

Museo de Arte Contemporáneo

Puente de San Martín

C. Sta. Ana

8 Sinagoga de Santa María la Blanca

4 San Antonio

Iglesia de Sant Tomé

Pl. de El Salvador

Taller del Moro
5
C. Taller del Moro

Casa-Museo El Greco **6**

Palacio de Fuensalida

7 Sinagoga del Tránsito
Pso. del Tránsito

Pso. S. Cristóbal

C. de S. Torculato

Río Tajo

Museo Victorio Macho

Cortes de Castilla-La-Mancha

Pl. del Calvario

Pl. San Cipriano

Carreras de San

1 Museo de Santa Cruz

2 Museo del Ejército (Alcázar)

3 Catedral

4 Iglesia de Sant Tomé

5 Café Del Fin

6 Casa-Museo El Greco

7 Sinagoga del Tránsito & Museo Sefardí

8 Sinagoga de Santa María la Blanca

9 Monasterio de San Juan de los Reyes

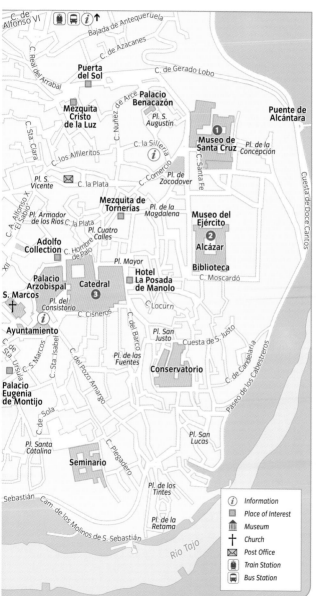

C. de Alfonso VI

Bajada de Antequeruela

C. de Azacanes

C. de Gerado Lobo

Puerta del Sol

C. Real del Arrabal

Mezquita Cristo de la Luz

Palacio Benacazón

Pl. S. Augustín

Puente de Alcántara

C. Nuñez de Arce

Museo de Santa Cruz ❶

Pl. de la Concepción

C. Sta. Clara

C. los Alfileritos

C. la Silleria

C. Comercio

C. Santa Fe

Cuesta de Doce Cantos

Pl. S. Vicente

C. la Plata

Pl. de Zocodover

Mezquita de Torrerías

Pl. de la Magdalena

Museo del Ejército ❷

C. A Alfonso X El Sabio

Pl. Armador de los Rios

C. la Plata

Alcázar

Pl. Cuatro Calles

Adolfo Collection

C. Hombre de Palo

Pl. Mayor

Biblioteca

C. Moscardó

Palacio Arzobispal

Catedral ❸

Hotel La Posada de Manolo

S. Marcos

Pl. del Consistorio

C. Cisneros

C. Locurn

Ayuntamiento

C. del Barco

Pl. San Justo

Cuesta de S. Justo

C. de Sta. Ursula

C. S. Marcos

C. Sta. Isabel

C. del pozo Amargo

Pl. de las Fuentes

C. de Candelaria

Paseo de los Cabestreros

Palacio Eugenia de Montijo

Conservatorio

C. de Sola

Pl. Santa Cátalina

C. Plegadero

Pl. San Lucas

Seminario

Pl. de los Tintes

Sebastián

Cam. de los Molinos de S. Sebastián

Pl. de la Retama

Río Tajo

ⓘ Information
◻ Place of Interest
🏛 Museum
✝ Church
✉ Post Office
🚆 Train Station
🚌 Bus Station

Toledo is a captivating city, coiled around a hilltop overlooking the River Tajo. Artist El Greco, who lived here for decades, never tired of painting its serene silhouette. The most striking monument is the huge cathedral, but the wealth of mosques and synagogues attest to Toledo's reputation for religious tolerance. START: **Train from Atocha Station (see Practical Matters, below). Trip length: 1 day.**

❶ ★ Museo de Santa Cruz.

The Renaissance Hospital de Santa Cruz is adorned with intricate Plateresque stonework. Now a fascinating museum with collections spanning everything from painting to archaeology, it is linked to the Prado, and often presents excellent temporary exhibitions. ⏱ 30 min. C/ Cervantes 3. ☎ 95-222-10-36. Free admission. Mon–Sat 10am–6:30pm, Sun 10am–2pm.

❷ ★ Museo del Ejército (Alcázar).

This huge 16th-century fortress was built first as a royal residence for Carlos I, but is better known to modern Spaniards for the terrible siege which resulted in its destruction during the Spanish Civil War. You can learn more about the siege, and about the fortress's long and violent history, in the national army museum, which has returned here

The 16th-century Alcázar.

after extensive restoration work. Displays also include archaeological finds dating back to the Bronze Age. ⏱ 1 hr. Cuesta de Carlos V. ☎ 92-522-88-00. www.ejercito.mde.es/en/. Adults 5€, concessions 2.50€. Free admission Sun 10am–3pm. Oct–May Tues–Sat 10am–7pm, Sun 10am–3pm; June–Sept Tues–Sat 10am–9pm, Sun 10am–3pm. Closed Mon.

❸ ★★★ Catedral.

Toledo's cathedral is considered the finest expression of the Gothic architectural style in Spain. It was begun in 1226, completed at the end of the 15th century, and further embellished in succeeding centuries. Like many churches of the period, it was built over the great mosque that once occupied the site. The cathedral is made of the palest stone, which seems to amplify the spacious interior, lit by 15th- and 16th-century **stained glass windows.** An enormous Gothic *retablo* dominates the **main altar,** theatrically lit by shafts of sunlight that enter through the cathedral's most extraordinary and unique feature, the **Transparente.** This surprising baroque concoction is a hole in the roof, around which stucco angels swirl. The **cloister,** with its lacy stonework, is quiet and contemplative. ⏱ 1 hr. C/ Cardenal Cisneros 1. ☎ 92-522-22-41. www.catedralprimada.es. Admission (includes museum) 7€. Mon–Sat 10am–6pm and Sun 2–6pm.

❹ ★★ Iglesia de Sant Tomé.

This was El Greco's parish church, and has won its place on every visitor's itinerary, thanks to a single painting: The Burial of the Count of

The decorated walls of the Sinagoga del Tránsito.

Orgaz, which El Greco painted for the church between 1586 and 1588. This huge canvas updates a popular local story about the 14th-century knight Don Gonzalo Ruíz, a famously pious and philanthropic man whose family would later become the Counts of Orgaz. It was said that, at his funeral, Saints Stephen and Augustine descended from heaven to bury him with their own hands. In El Greco's version, the onlookers at the funeral (which include a self-portrait of the artist) are lifelike portrayals of notable Toledanos of the time. ⏱ *30 min. Plaza del Conde 4.* ☎ *92-525-60-98. www.santotome.org. Admission 1.90€ adults, 1.40€ under-18s and*

Toledo's Gothic Cathedral.

seniors. June–Sept Mon–Sat 10am–6:45pm; Oct–May Mon–Sat 10am–5:45pm, Sun 10am–2pm.

5 **Café Del Fin.** This bright, modern cafe has sofas, local artworks, and a menu of simple dishes such as pastas and sandwiches, as well as free Wi-Fi. *C/ Taller del Moro 1.* ☎ *92-525-10-52. www.cafedelfin. com. Set lunch 10€.*

6 ★ **Casa-Museo El Greco.** It is unlikely that El Greco (1541–1614) actually lived in this 16th-century mansion, but his home was probably very similar. The rooms are filled with period furnishings, including some colorful ceramic tiles, and serve as a backdrop to a fine collection of the artist's work. I always particularly enjoy the scenes of Toledo, which remain surprisingly unchanged. ⏱ *45 min. C/ Samuel Leví s/n.* ☎ *92-522-44-05. http://en.museodelgreco.mcu. es. Adults 5€, free for 65 and over and children 17 and under. Free admission Sat after 4pm and Sun. Apr–May Tues–Sat 9:30am–8:30pm, Sun 10am–3pm; Oct–Mar Tues–Sat 9:30am–6:30pm, Sun 10am–3pm.*

7 ★ **Sinagoga del Tránsito & Museo Sefardí.** One of Toledo's trio of surviving synagogues is now a museum dedicated to Jewish culture. The Jews were expelled from

Practical Matters—Toledo

By car from Madrid, take the A42 highway to Toledo; the distance is 89km (55 miles). **Avant trains** (☎ 90-232-03-20; www.renfe.com) leave at least hourly from Madrid's Atocha station, taking 30 minutes. **Tourist Information Offices** are at Puerta de Bisagra (☎ 92-522-08-43) and Plaza del Consistorio 1 (☎ 92-525-40-30; www.toledo-turismo.org).

To stay overnight, **Hotel La Posada de Manolo,** Calle Sixto Ramón Parro 8 (☎ 92-528-22-50; www.laposadademanolo.com), is a small, charming guesthouse; doubles cost 70€ to 85€. **Palacio Eugenia de Montijo,** Plaza Juego de Pelota 7 (☎ 92-527-46-90; www.hotel-palacioeugeniademontijo.com), is a stylish boutique hotel with a tiny spa. Doubles range from 120€ to 200€.

Adolfo Collection 1924, Calle Nuncio Viejo 1 (☎ 92-522-42-24), offers gourmet tapas and fine wines. **Hostal del Cardenal,** Paseo de Recadero 24 (☎ 92-522-08-62), in an 18th-century *palacete*, specializes in classic Castilian cuisine.

Spain in 1492, but previously Toledo had been home to one of the largest Jewish communities on the peninsula. The Sinagoga del Tránsito was built in the 13th century with funds raised by Samuel Leví, financier to Pedro the Cruel (who eventually had Samuel tortured to death). The synagogue is a jewel of Mudéjar architecture, with a magnificent gilded ceiling and horseshoe arches. 🕐 *30 min. C/ Samuel Leví.* ☎ *92-522-36-65. http:// museosefardi.mcu.es. Adults 3€, free for 65 and over and children 17 and under. Free admission Sat after 2pm and Sun. Tues–Sat 9:30am– 7pm, Sun 10am–2pm. Closed Mon.*

8 ★ **Sinagoga de Santa María la Blanca.** The Sinagoga de Santa María la Blanca, built in the late 12th century, was also converted into a church after the expulsion of the Jews. Fortunately, its serene ranks of pale stucco horseshoe arches have been untouched through the centuries, and this remains one of my favorite places in the city. 🕐 *30 min. C/ de los Reyes Católicos 4.* ☎ *92-522-72-57. Admission 2.30€. Daily 10am–6pm.*

9 ★ **Monasterio de San Juan de los Reyes.** Another corner I love in this beautiful city is the historic cloister of this monastery, particularly in spring when the orange trees are in bloom. 🕐 *30 min. C/ de los Reyes Católicos 2.* ☎ *92-522-38-02. www.sanjuandelosreyes.org. Admission 2.30€. Daily 10am– 5:45pm, until 7pm in summer.* ●

Monasterio de San Juan de los Reyes.

The
Savvy Traveler

Before You Go

Spanish Government Tourist Offices

In the U.S.: 60 East 42nd St., Suite 5300, New York, NY 10165-0039 (☎ **212/265-8822**); 8383 Wilshire Blvd., Suite 965, Beverly Hills, CA 90211 (☎ **323/658-7188**); 845 N. Michigan Ave., Suite 915E, Chicago, IL 60611 (☎ **312/642-1992**); and 1395 Brickell Ave., Suite 1130, Miami, FL 33131 (☎ **305/358-1992**). **In Canada:** 2 Bloor St. W., 34th Floor, Toronto, Ontario M4W 3E2 (☎ **416/961-3131**). **In the U.K.:** 79 New Cavendish St., London W1W 6XB (☎ **0800/10-10-50-50**). www.spain.info.

The Best Times to Go

April to early June and **September to late October** are the best times to visit Madrid, when the sky is bright blue but temperatures are moderate. In **May,** the best traditional festival takes place in honor of the city's patron saint, San Isidro. I love the city in **June,** when the flowers are blooming in the parks and the Madrileños take to the streets. In hot and sweaty **August,** much of the city shuts down as its citizens head for the beaches. Many shops and restaurants close for the entire month, so be sure to call in advance. However, this is also when some of the best traditional festivals are held, including La Paloma. **November** to **February** is surprisingly cold, but you'll have the city to yourself, and prices drop for hotels and flights. The **Christmas** season in Madrid, beginning in early **December** and extending through the 1st week of **January,** is especially festive.

As Spain's capital, Madrid is a popular year-round destination. It is also a major international trade fair

Previous page: Carousel, Calle Serrano.

and conference destination throughout the year, so mid- to high-range hotels should be booked well in advance.

Festivals & Special Events

SPRING. **Semana Santa (Easter Week)** is a relatively low-key festival in Madrid, compared to the great Andalucian cities, but is still celebrated with solemn processions. The Easter celebrations in **Toledo** are splendid, particularly on Holy Thursday and Good Friday. May 1 is **May Day,** or Labor Day, and the streets are full of marching trade-union members. **May 2 (Día de la Comunidad)** is a public holiday, in commemoration of the Madrileño uprising against Napoleonic troops in 1808. It's celebrated with outdoor concerts and traditional dancing on the Plaza del Dos de Mayo, and a military parade through the center. The city's biggest festival, the **Fiesta de San Isidro,** a colorful and electrifying spectacle of traditional dance, street parties, concerts, and special events, takes place for 2 weeks around May 15. During **Corpus Christi,** which falls in either late May or early June, the streets of Toledo are carpeted in flowers and a glittering procession takes place in the heart of the old city.

SUMMER. The **Fiesta de San Antonio de la Florida** (June 13) is a delightfully old-fashioned neighborhood festival, with bunting, street parties, and a pilgrimage to the saint's church, which was frescoed by Goya. During the **Noche de Sant Juan** (June 23), Madrid celebrates the summer solstice with fireworks and bonfires in the Parque del Retiro. There are numerous music festivals held in June and July, but the great summer cultural festival is **Veranos de la Villa** (July–Aug; http://veranosdelavilla.esmadrid.com/), which has everything from classical drama to contemporary dance at the city's top venues. August is a wonderful month for *castizo* ("genuine") neighborhood festivals, held in honor of their patron saints. The best of these are **La Paloma** in La Latina (Aug 15), **San Lorenzo** in Lavapiés (Aug 10), and **San Cayetano** in Cascorro (Aug 7). Celebrations continue for about a week on either side of the saint's feast day. **Assumption Day** (Aug 15) is a public holiday.

FALL. The **Romeria de Nuestra Señora Virgen de Gracia,** a pilgrimage that culminates in a huge group picnic, takes place in San Lorenzo de Escorial on the second Sunday of September. The **Noche Blanca** is a wide-ranging cultural festival, with free events across the city during the night of September 23, including circus performances, music concerts, and free access to most municipal museums.

WINTER. **All Saints' Day** (Nov 1), a public holiday, is reverently celebrated: Relatives and friends visit the graves of loved ones and eat traditional foods. Madrid has two patron saints: San Isidro, whose fiesta is celebrated in May, and the **Virgen de la Almudena,** whose feast day (Nov 9) is marked with 2 weeks of festivities. The weeks leading to **Navidad** (Christmas) are marked by Christmas fairs in the Plaza Mayor (the largest) and several other squares throughout the historic center, selling handicrafts, Christmas decorations, trees, and Nativity figurines (for their *belenes*—nativity dioramas). The city council erects its own nativity scene in the Plaza de la Villa, in front of the city hall. **Día de los Reyes** (Three Kings' Day), January 6, remains the traditional Catholic celebration of Christmas gift-giving (even though Santa Claus has made inroads and many families now exchange gifts on Dec 25). On the previous evening, public celebrations take place in cities and towns across Spain; in Madrid, the main parade is led by three costumed Magi who parade through the Plaza Mayor throwing candy to children. **Carnaval** (just prior to Lent) is low-key in Madrid, with dressing up only by groups of children or stall owners in the local markets.

The Weather

Madrid is set on a high plateau in the center of Spain—which means

AVERAGE TEMPERATURE & RAINFALL IN MADRID				
	°C	°F	RAINFALL IN MM	INCHES
Jan	9	49	33	1.3
Feb	11	52	34	1.3
March	15	59	23	.9
April	18	65	39	1.5
May	21	70	47	1.8
June	27	81	26	1
July	31	88	11	.4
Aug	30	86	12	.5
Sep	25	77	24	.9
Oct	19	66	39	1.5
Nov	13	56	48	1.9
Dec	9	49	48	1.9

Useful Websites

www.ctm-madrid.es: The city's official transportation website, with information (in English) on local trains, buses, and the Metro system.

www.esmadrid.com: The city's official tourism site, in several languages, with flashy graphics and plenty of useful information for business and leisure travelers. Can be hard to find what you're looking for.

www.munimadrid.es: Useful, city-run website with practical information on the city's main sights, parks, sports facilities, and more. In Spanish only.

www.okspain.org: Tourist Office of Spain official U.S. site; it has detailed "Before You Travel" information (including U.S. air connections).

www.renfe.com: The official site for Spanish rail travel, with routes, schedules, and online booking.

searingly hot summers and bitterly cold winters. As a local saying goes, the capital endures "nine months of winter and three months of hell." However, even the coldest days are usually sunny, with the skies beautiful and bright, just as they were immortalized in Goya's great paintings. Rain usually falls in short but intense, thundery bursts, particularly in April and October, so come prepared. In July and August, the temperatures regularly soar well above 30°C (86°F), without a breath of wind to keep you cool. However, air-conditioned museums, restaurants, and hotels can keep the worst of the heat at bay. Copy the locals and retire to your room for a siesta, emerging once the worst of the heat has passed.

Cellphones (móviles)

World phones—or GSM (Global System for Mobiles)—are the standard in Spain (and most of the world). If your cellphone is on a GSM system, and you have a world-capable multiband phone, you can make and receive calls from Spain. Just call your operator and ask for "international roaming" to be activated. You can also rent a GSM phone (see below), but it may work out cheaper to simply buy a pay-as you-go phone once in Madrid. The main Spanish networks are Movistar, Vodafone, Orange, and Yoigo; the latter is usually the cheapest. You will need to take a passport or driving license to purchase a phone. These are available from the department stores **El Corte Inglés,** Calle Preciados 3 (☎ **91-379-80-00**), and **FNAC,** Calle Preciados 28 (☎ **91-595-61-00**), among many. You can usually buy a simple phone for around 50€, which usually includes around 20€ of credit. It is also possible to buy a Spanish SIM card (for around 15€) for your own phone, but check with your operator to ensure that your phone is unlocked. North Americans can rent a GSM phone before leaving home from **InTouch USA** (☎ **800/872-7626;** www.intouchglobal.com) or **Road-Post** (☎ **888/290-1616** or 905/272-4934; www.roadpost.com).

Car Rentals

Driving in Madrid isn't advised, especially with the preponderance of inexpensive taxi and Metro services. The day trips we have suggested are all easily accessible by public transportation, although it is easier to combine visits (for example, visiting both Aranjuez and Toledo in a single day) if you rent a car. North America's biggest car-rental companies, including Avis, Budget, and Hertz, maintain offices in Madrid, including at Barajas airport and the Atocha and Chamartin rail stations. The best deals can usually be found on the Internet, so shop around before coming. Useful contact details include: **Avis** ☎ 800/331-1212 (U.S.), ☎ 08445/818-181 (U.K.), ☎ 90-213-55-31 (Spain); www.avis.com; **Hertz** ☎ 800/654-3131 (U.S.), ☎ 08708/44-88-44 (U.K.), ☎ 90-240-24-05 (Spain); www.hertz.com; and **EuropCar** ☎ 877/940-6900 (U.S.), ☎ 0871/308-1087 (U.K.); ☎ 91-722-62-00 or 91-343-45-12 (Spain); www.europcar.com. Spanish company **Pepecar** (☎ 80-741-42-43; www.pepecar.com) offers low-cost car rental in Madrid.

Getting **There**

By Plane

From Madrid's **Barajas** airport (12km/7½ miles from the city center), there are several ways to get into town. The most convenient is the **Metro** (line 8), with stations at Terminals 2 (also for Terminals 1 and 3) and 4. Single tickets cost 2€ (note that public transportation passes require payment of a supplement of 1€ for journeys to and from the airport). The **express airport bus** (2€; buy ticket on the bus) connects with Atocha train station, with a stop at Plaza de Cibeles. **Local bus** services link the airport with the **Avenida de América** bus station in northeast Madrid (which is also on the Metro network). Take bus No. 200 from Terminals 1, 2, or 3, or bus No. 204 from Terminal 4. Tickets cost 1€. Taxis leave from outside all terminals. A journey to the city center shouldn't cost more than 30€, including airport and luggage supplements. Ask for a receipt.

By Car

Several major highways converge on Madrid, which lies at the very center of Spain. Highway **A2** leads to Zaragoza and Barcelona in the northeast, and the **A3** heads directly east to Valencia. The **A6** runs northwest toward Galicia (take this for Segovia and Ávila), and the **A5** heads southwest toward Extremadura and Seville. The **A42** is a direct highway to Toledo. The city is encircled by three major ring roads: the **M30,** the **M40,** and the **M50.** Traffic is very sluggish, particularly during rush hour, when it regularly slows to a standstill.

By Train

Most national (RENFE; www.renfe.com) and international trains arrive at **Atocha,** Glorieta del Emperador Carlos V (☎ 91-468-83-32; Metro: Atocha), or **Chamartín,** Calle Augustín de Foxa s/n (☎ 91-468-83-32; Metro: Chamartín) in the north. **Atocha** is the biggest station in Spain, and the terminal for the AVE high-speed rail links with Barcelona and Seville.

Getting **Around**

By Metro

The **Metro** (☎ 90-244-44-03; www.metromadrid.es) is Madrid's efficient, modern, and clean subway (underground rail) system. The extensive network (12 color-coded lines, plus the "R" Ópera-to-Príncipe Pío link) makes it the fastest and easiest way to navigate the city. Red diamond symbols with a blue Metro sign mark stations. Single-ticket fares (*sencillo*) are 1€, although you can get a **Metrobús pass** (good for 10 trips on the Metro or the bus) for 9.30€, from vending machines in Metro stations. This is usually better value than the tourist passes (*abono turístico*), which are valid for unlimited travel for periods of between 1 and 7 days (1-day pass 6€, 2 days 10€, 3 days 13€, 5 days 19€, 7 days 25€, with a 50% discount for children under 11). The Metro operates daily 6am to 2am, with fewer services on Sundays.

By Taxi

Taxis, which are white with a red diagonal stripe on the front doors, are plentiful and reasonably priced; few journeys cost more than 10€. You can either hail a cab in the street (the green light on the roof means it's available) or grab one where they're lined up (usually outside hotels). There are also taxi ranks at the two main train stations, Atocha and Chamartín, and at several city-center locations, including the Plaza Isabel II and the Plaza del Callao (on the Gran Vía). Taxi ranks are identified with a blue sign emblazoned with the white letter "T." Fares begin at 2.10€ (2.20€ at night), with supplements for journeys to and from the airport and rail or bus stations. There is no supplement for luggage or the transport of wheelchairs. Note that if you order a taxi by phone, you will also pay for the time it takes for it to arrive at your call-out point. Reliable taxi companies include **Radio Taxi** (☎ 91-447-51-80) and **Tele-taxi** (☎ 91-371-21-31). **Euro Taxi** has specially adapted taxis for the disabled; book in advance (☎ 91-547-85-00).

By Bus

Buses are plentiful and convenient, but occasionally frustratingly slow because of the high volume of traffic on the city streets. On the plus side, they are refreshingly air-conditioned in summer. Night buses (called *búhos*, meaning "owls" operate between approximately 11:20pm and 5:30am. The *Metrobúho* is a night bus service that follows the routes of the Metro lines from 12:45am to 5:45am at weekends. Single tickets (buy from the driver) for bus journeys, including night buses, cost 1€, although the Metrobús pass (see above) offers the best value.

By Car

Trying to negotiate Madrid's unfamiliar, traffic-clogged streets can be nerve-racking, and parking is an expensive nightmare. The day trips I've described in this book—Toledo, El Escorial, and Aranjuez—are all easy to do by public transportation. However, a car is useful if you plan to combine out-of-town day trips, or simply want to explore the surrounding countryside at your leisure. There are several central underground parking lots, including at Plaza del Sol, Plaza de España, and several locations on the Gran Vía. These charge approximately 2.50€ per hour, with a maximum charge of 28.90€ for 24 hours. Note that you must also pay if you park on the street: Blue and green dotted lines denote parking spaces. Prices are from 1.80€ per hour in a green zone, and from 2.60€ for 2 hours in a blue zone. Very few hotels offer private parking; ask before booking.

On Foot
Strolling in central Madrid is a pastime verging on an art form, and the compact city is ideal for walking, especially in the atmospheric maze of the old center near the Plaza Mayor. The wide avenues of Salamanca may be shopping heaven, but it can be a bit of a slog getting around this extensive neighborhood.

Fast **Facts**

APARTMENT RENTALS   Among the options are: **Friendly Rentals** (☎ **93-268-80-51;** www.friendly rentals.com), which has stylish properties at surprisingly good prices; **www.spain-select.com**, which offers luxurious apartments in the city's smartest neighborhoods; and **www.rentmadrid.es**, with a choice of properties in the old center.

ATMS/CASHPOINTS   Maestro, Cirrus, and Visa cards are readily accepted at all ATMs. Exchange currency at banks or *casas de cambio* (exchange houses). Banks usually offer the best deals, but *casas de cambio* are open later. They usually charge hefty commission rates, so check before you make any transactions. You can also find currency-exchange offices at the Atocha rail station and Barajas airport. Major Spanish banks include Caja de Madrid, BBVA, and Santander. Branches of these are located near the Plaza Mayor and along the Gran Vía. Most banks offer 24-hour ATMs: These are usually the best way to access local currency in Spain, but check overseas transaction rates with your home bank.

BUSINESS HOURS   Banks are open Monday to Friday 8:30am to 2pm. Most offices are open Monday to Friday from 9am to 6 or 7pm (in July, 8am–3pm). In August, businesses are generally on skeleton staff, if not closed altogether. At restaurants, lunch is usually from 1:30 or 2 to 4pm and dinner 9 to 11:30pm or midnight. Major retail stores are open Monday to Saturday from 9:30 or 10am to 8pm, with many stores in shopping malls also opening on the first Sunday of the month; staff at smaller establishments, however, often still close for siesta in the mid-afternoon, doing business from 9:30am to 2pm and 4:30 to 8 or 8:30pm.

DOCTORS   Dial ☎ **112** in any emergency, including medical emergencies. The old local number (used before the introduction of the pan-European emergency number, 112), ☎ **061,** is still valid. For information on local doctors, call the city information line on ☎ **012.**

ELECTRICITY   Hotels operate on 220 volts AC. The El Corte Inglés department store, Calle Preciados 3 (☎ **91-379-80-00**), sells international adaptors.

EMBASSIES   **U.S.A.,** Calle Serrano 75, Salamanca (☎ **91-587-22-00**); **Canada,** Torre Espacio, Paseo de la Castellana 259D (☎ **91-382-84-00**); **U.K.,** Torre Espacio, Paseo de la Castellana 259D (☎ **91-714-63-00**); **Australia,** Torre Espacio, Paseo de la Castellana 259D (☎ **91-353-66-00**); **New Zealand,** Calle Pinar 7 (☎ **91-523-02-26**).

EMERGENCIES   For all emergencies, call the pan-European emergency telephone number, ☎ 112, although the old numbers still function: ☎ 061 for ambulance and ☎ 080 for fire.

GAY & LESBIAN TRAVELERS   In 1978, Spain legalized homosexuality among consenting adults, and in 1995, Spain banned discrimination based on sexual orientation. Marriage between same-sex couples became legal in 2005. Madrid is one of the major centers of gay life in Spain, with the vibrant neighborhood of Chueca the capital of the gay scene. You'll find shops, bars, restaurants, hotels, and more clustered in this area. Across the rest of the city, the gay scene is less visible than in other Spanish destinations such as Barcelona or Sitges. The websites **www.gayinspain.com** and **www.chueca.com** have detailed and destination-specific listings for gay travelers.

HOLIDAYS   Holidays observed include: January 1 (New Year's Day), January 6 (Feast of the Epiphany), March/April (Good Friday), May 1 (May Day), May 2 (Fiesta de la Comunidad), August 15 (Feast of the Assumption), October 12 (Spain's National Day), November 1 (All Saints' Day), December 6 (Constitution Day), December 8 (Feast of the Immaculate Conception), and December 25 (Christmas).

INSURANCE   Check your existing insurance policies before you buy travel insurance to cover trip cancellation, lost luggage, medical expenses, or car rental insurance. For travel overseas, most U.S. health plans (including Medicare and Medicaid) do not provide coverage, and the ones that do often require payment up front for services. **Canadians** should check with their provincial health plan offices or call **Health Canada** (☎ 866/225-0709; www.hc-sc.gc.ca) to find out the extent of their coverage and what documentation and receipts they must take home in case they are treated overseas.

Travelers from the **U.K. and Eire** should carry their European Health Insurance Card (EHIC; ☎ 0845/606-2030; www.ehic.org.uk). Note, however, that the EHIC only covers "necessary medical treatment," and for repatriation costs, lost money, baggage, or cancellation, travel insurance from a reputable company should always be sought.

INTERNET   Internet access is plentiful, both in cybercafes (Internet cafes or *cibercafes*) and frequently in hotels, several of which now offer Wi-Fi. The **Café Comercial,** Glorieta Bilbao 7 (☎ 91-521-56-55), is old and atmospheric and has a couple of creaky terminals. There are numerous *locutorios* (phone centers) clustered around the Puerta del Sol, where you can make cheap international calls and usually get online at several terminals. **Workcenter** (the branch at Plaza Canalejas is the most convenient; find more branches at www.workcenter.es) has a wide range of business and printing services, as well as fast Internet access.

LOST PROPERTY   Call credit card companies the minute you discover your wallet has been lost or stolen, and file a report at the nearest police precinct. Your credit card company or insurer will almost certainly require a police report number or record. **Visa's** emergency number in Spain is ☎ 90-099-11-24. **American Express** cardholders and traveler's check holders should call ☎ 90-237-56-37 in Spain. **MasterCard** holders should call ☎ 90-097-12-31 in Spain.

MAIL & POSTAGE   Spanish post offices are called *correos* (koh-*ray*-os), and are identified by yellow-and-white signs with a crown and the words *Correos y Telégrafos*. Main offices are generally open 9am to 8pm Monday to Friday and Saturday 9am to 7pm. The Central Post Office is at Paseo del Prado 1 (☎ 91-523-06-94). Other branches are at Carrera de San Francisco 13, Calle Mejia Lequerica 7, and Plaza Oriente s/n.

MONEY   The single European currency in Spain is the **euro.** At press time, the exchange rate was approximately 1€ = US$1.42 or £0.87. For up-to-the-minute exchange rates between the euro and the dollar, check the currency converter website **www.xe.com/ucc**.

PASSPORTS   No visas are required for U.S. or Canadian passport holders traveling to Spain, providing your stay does not exceed 90 days. Australian visitors do need a visa. If your passport is lost or stolen, contact your country's embassy or consulate immediately; see "Embassies," above. Make a copy of your passport's critical pages and keep it separately from your passport.

PHARMACIES   Pharmacies *(farmacias)* operate during normal business hours, and in every district one remains open all night and on public holidays. The location and phone number of this *farmacia de guardia* is posted on the door of all the other pharmacies. A couple of central pharmacies open 24/7 include **Farmacia de la Paloma,** Calle Toledo 46 (☎ 91-365-34-58; www.farmaciadelapaloma.com), and **Farmacia del Globo,** Calle Atocha 46 (☎ 91-369-20-00). You can also call the city information line ☎ 012 for the addresses of all-night pharmacies.

POLICE   For all emergencies, call ☎ 112. The old numbers (which existed prior to the introduction of the pan-European emergency number) still work too: national police ☎ 091 and local police ☎ 092.

SAFETY   Violent crime in Madrid is a rarity, but petty criminals frequent tourist areas and major attractions such as museums, restaurants, hotels, trains, stations, airports, subways, and ATMs. Exercise care around major tourist sights, especially around the Plaza Mayor, the Gran Vía, and the neighborhoods of Lavapiés and La Latina. Be especially careful of pickpockets on the Metro, and do not allow flower-bearing gypsies to approach you anywhere. Be equally careful of young women and children bearing clipboards with fake sponsorship forms: This is a common scam to pick your pockets. Do not enter any of the public parks after nightfall. **SATE** (Servicio de Atención al Turista Extranjero or Tourist Attention Service), Calle Leganitos 19 (☎ 91-548-85-37), has English-speaking attendants who can aid crime victims in reporting losses and obtaining new documents. The office is open 9am to midnight.

SMOKING   A law banning smoking in public places, including on public transportation and in offices and hospitals, was enacted in early 2006, and extended to all bars, restaurants, and nightclubs in 2011.

TAXES   Value-added tax (VAT), known in Spain as IVA, ranges from 4% to 18%, depending on the commodity being sold. Food, wine, and basic necessities are taxed at 8%; most goods and services (including car rentals) at 18%; and hotels at 8%. Non-E.U. residents are entitled to a reimbursement of the 18% IVA on most purchases worth more than 90.15€ made at shops offering "Tax Free" or "Global Refund" shopping. Forms, obtained from the store where you made your purchase, must be stamped at Customs upon departure. For more information, see **www.globalrefund.com**.

TELEPHONES   For national telephone information, dial ☎ **11888.** For international telephone information, call ☎ **11886.** You can make international calls from booths identified with the word *Internacional.* To make an international call, dial ☎ **00,** wait for the tone, and dial the country code, area code, and number. If you're making a local call within Madrid, you must still dial Madrid's two-digit city code **(91)** first, and then the seven-digit number. To make a long-distance call within Spain, the procedure is the same, except that you dial the prefix of the city you're calling.

TIPPING   More expensive restaurants add 8% tax and cheaper ones incorporatethe taxes into their prices. This is *not* a service charge, and a tip of 5% to 10% is expected from tourists in these establishments, although locals rarely leave more than a couple of euros. For coffee and snacks most people just leave a few coins or round up to the nearest euro. Taxis do not expect tips, although they might hope for something from tourists. Tip hotel porters and doormen 1€ and maids about the same amount per day.

TOILETS   In Spain they're called *aseos, servicios,* or *lavabos,* and are labeled *señores, hombres,* or *caballeros* for men, and *damas* or *señoras* for women.

TOURIST INFORMATION   **Turismo de Madrid,** Plaza Mayor 27 (☎ **91-588-16-36;** www.esmadrid.com), is run by the city council and offers a wealth of information as well as useful maps and an excellent free monthly magazine, *esMadridmagazine,* with event listings. For information on the city plus the surrounding area (the Comunidad de Madrid) visit the **Oficina de Turismo de la Comunidad de Madrid,** Calle Duque de Medinaceli 2 (☎ **91-429-49-51**). Tourism information offices are also at Atocha train station and the airport. Call ☎ **010** for general visitor information.

TRAVELERS WITH DISABILITIES   Much of Madrid is steep and even cobbled in some areas, making it awkward for wheelchair users. Many of the older buildings have stairs, making it difficult for visitors with disabilities to get around, although conditions are slowly improving. Newer hotels are more sensitive to the needs of persons with disabilities, and more expensive restaurants are generally wheelchair-accessible. The city tourism website, www.esmadrid.com, has lists of accessible museums, hotels, and shops, and also provides updates on new services being introduced for disabled travelers. These include special guided tours—currently offered in Spanish only, but it is hoped that other languages will be introduced. (The website is not easy to navigate: Go to "Always," then click "Guide," which brings up the Accessible Madrid option.) You might consider taking an organized tour specifically designed for disabled travelers. In the U.S., **Flying Wheels Travel** (☎ **507/451-5005;** www.flying wheelstravel.com) sometimes offers escorted tours to Spain, and **Access-Able Travel Source** (☎ **303/232-2979;** www.access-able.com) has access information for people traveling to Madrid (as well as other worldwide destinations). Pick up a **Metro** plan (also available at www.metromadrid.es), which indicates stations with elevators and wheelchair access. All **buses** (www.emtmadrid.es) are equipped for wheelchairs, although it is advisable to travel off-peak rather than fight your way through the crowds. All sightseeing buses (Madrid Vision) can accommodate wheelchairs. **Famma,** Calle Galileo 69 (☎ **91-593-35-50;** www.famma.org), a federation of private organizations for the disabled, produces an excellent comprehensive guide (in Spanish only) to accessibility in Madrid. It is available online. It includes accessibility appraisals of shops, hotels, theaters, and bus and rail stations, among other institutions.

Madrid: **A Brief History**

CA.1000 B.C. The first settlements in the Madrid area grow up along the Manzanares river.

A.D. 412 The Goths make Toledo their capital.

711 The Moors invade the Iberian peninsula.

CA. 860 The Arabic fortress of Mayrit (possibly the origin "Madrid") is established where the Royal Palace currently stands.

1083 Christian armies capture Madrid.

1202 Madrid is declared a free city in a statute issued by Alfonso VIII.

1309 The itinerant Spanish *Cortes* (parliament) is held in Madrid for the first time.

1492 Ferdinand and Isabella (the "Catholic Monarchs") defeat Granada, the last Moorish kingdom on the Iberian peninsula. The Jews are expelled from Spain. Christopher Columbus reaches the Americas.

1495 A royal marriage unites the Spanish monarchs with the Austrian Habsburg Emperors.

1520 Castilian towns, including Madrid, join the *Comunero* revolt against Carlos I.

1561 Felipe II declares Madrid the first permanent capital of Spain. Numerous building projects are initiated.

1600–06 Madrid is briefly replaced by Valladolid as Spanish capital.

1620 Plaza Mayor is completed.

1700 Carlos II dies without an heir; Felipe V is crowned the first Bourbon king of Spain.

1701–13 The Spanish War of Succession rips across the country.

1734 The Royal Palace is destroyed by a huge blaze.

1808 Napoleonic troops take Madrid, despite heroic resistance by Madrileños. Carlos IV abdicates, and Napoleon appoints his brother Joseph as King of Spain.

1813 The Spanish monarchy is restored under Fernando VII.

1833–34 First Carlist Wars. Supporters of Isabel II defeat the pretender Don Carlos.

1836 Mendizabel laws appropriate church property for the state.

1868 General Primo de Rivera declares the First Republic, triggering the Second Carlist War. Isabel II flees from Spain.

1876 Spanish monarchy once again restored under Alfonso XII.

1908 Work begins on the Gran Vía.

1923 General Primo de Rivera declares his dictatorship, but is forced to resign 6 years later in the face of major economic problems.

1931 Spain votes overwhelmingly for a Republic and Alfonso XIII is forced to abdicate.

1936–9 Spanish Civil War. Madrid is the last city to fall to the Nationalists under Franco.

1975 Death of Franco and the coronation of Juan Carlos I.

1977 The Socialists win the first democratic elections in Spain since the Civil War. The following year, a new Spanish Constitution is signed.

1981 A right-wing military coup is foiled.

1980S The *Movida*, a socio-cultural movement that exploded across the city after the death of Franco, reaches its height. Alternative films, fashion, music, and art flourish.

1986 Spain joins the European Union (E.U.).

1992 Madrid is European Capital of Culture.

1996 Conservative Partido Popular (PP) wins general election.

2004 Terrorist attacks in Madrid claim the lives of 191 people. In the face of criticism over their handling of the crisis, the PP is ousted in the general election and the leader of the Spanish Socialist Party (PSOE), José Luis Rodríguez Zapatero, becomes Prime Minister of Spain.

2005 The Reina Sofía is dramatically enlarged by Jean Nouvel.

2007 The Prado unveils its new extension by Rafael Moneo.

2008 Zapatero's Socialist government wins a second term of office in the general election. A tragic plane accident at Barajas airport kills 154 people.

2011 Popular anti-government protests against political corruption and the mishandling of the global crisis lead to huge, peaceful sit-ins in the Puerta del Sol and other squares. The incumbent Socialist Party is defeated in regional elections.

Madrid's **Architecture**

Moorish & Mudéjar (10th–13th C. A.D.)

Few vestiges of the old Arabic citadel survive, aside from a small stretch of the **old wall** in a shabby park near the Catedral de la Almudena. The Moors who converted and stayed behind after the Reconquest continued to work for their new Christian rulers, and their art, which fuses Arabic and European techniques, is known as *Mudéjar*. The little Mudéjar church of **San Nicolás** preserves a minaret from the mosque that once occupied the spot, neatly capped and turned into a bell tower. There are much finer examples of Mudéjar craftsmanship in Toledo, including the brilliant **Sinagoga del Tránsito.**

Gothic & Plateresque (15th–16th C.)

The best example of the Gothic style in the Madrid region (and one of the finest in all of Spain) is Toledo's majestic **cathedral,** with its pointed arches, elaborate sculptural decoration, and soaring vaults. Almost all the Gothic constructions in Madrid were destroyed, although the **Torre de los Lujanes** survives on the Plaza de la Villa. On this same square, the **Casa de Cisneros** features the delicate, intricate decorative stonework typical of

Plateresque architecture, which derives its name from the *plateros* or silversmiths.

Renaissance & Baroque (16th–18th c.)

Madrid's Golden Age in terms of historic architecture was the 17th century, when many of its most emblematic buildings were erected. The enormous palace at **El Escorial** is an elegantly restrained masterpiece by Juan Bautista de Toledo and his gifted collaborator, Juan de Herrera, whose penchant for austere lines is echoed in the designs for the **Plaza Mayor,** completed in 1620 by one of his pupils. The **Monasterio de la Encarnación** and the **Monasterio de las Descalzes Reales** are both refined early-baroque edifices, as is the **Casa de la Villa** (city hall). By the 18th century, baroque architecture was becoming more fulsome and lavish. Spanish monarchs invited Italian architects to design the new **Palacio Real (Royal Palace),** which remains the city's largest and most opulent baroque construction.

Neoclassicism, Eclecticism, Historicism (mid-18th–late-19th c.)

Under Carlos III and his Enlightenment ideals, the city was dramatically expanded and rebuilt. Architects sought inspiration in the cultures of Ancient Rome and Greece, adorning their buildings with classical columns and favoring straight, rational lines over the fanciful loops of the baroque. New projects included the majestic **Prado,** one of the first purpose-built museums in Europe, and the original hospital, which now contains the **Reina Sofía** museum. The pretty little **Observatory,** tucked away in a corner of the Retiro Park, is a jewel of neoclassical architecture. The splendid **Cibeles fountain,** with its depiction of the ancient goddess in her chariot, is another fine example of Neoclassicism. Toward the end of the 19th century, Neoclassicism began to merge with Eclecticism and Historicism as architects conflated various styles and influences in single buildings. The best examples of this type of architecture can be found in the first swathe of buildings built along the **Gran Vía,** at the junction with Calle Alcalá, where edifices clearly inspired by the French Second Empire rub shoulders with restrained neoclassical mansions.

Modern & Contemporary (early 20th c.–present)

The first buildings of the Gran Vía were erected in the 1st decade of the 20th century—grand, showy, and designed to demonstrate to the world that Madrid was a forward-thinking, modern capital. This street, like no other, captures the architectural trends of the century that followed. As the Gran Vía spreads slowly west, the buildings unfold like a textbook of 20th-century Madrileño architecture. There are very few buildings in the Art Nouveau style (called *Modernisme* in Spain) in the city, although the **Sociedad de Autores,** just north of the Gran Vía, is a remarkable exception. However, Art Deco was extremely popular, inspired in part by the startling new skyscrapers mushrooming in the big North American cities. The Gran Vía boasts several sensuously curved, Art Deco monuments, including the **Edificio Carrión** and the **Palacio de la Prensa** on the Plaza del Callao. The Franco years saw virtually no modern architecture of note, apart from a couple of skyscrapers remarkable only for their height. Architecture was little better served in the post-Franco era, with a clutch of banks and business towers such as the

Puerta de Europa, a pair of sky-scrapers leaning toward each other, completed in 1996. The greatest critical successes of the early 21st century have all been transforma-tions of existing buildings. Rafael Moneo's glassy expansion of the **Prado** (2007), Jean Nouvel's striking new addition to the **Reina Sofía** (2005), and Herzog & De Meuron's clever conversion of a factory into the **CaixaForum** have raised the city's profile considerably. The most dramatic new addition to the city skyline was completed in 2008: The Cuatro Torres (Four Towers) busi-ness district, composed of the four tallest skyscrapers in Spain, incud-ing Cesar Pelli's Crystal Tower.

Useful **Phrases**

Key Words & Phrases

ENGLISH	SPANISH	PRONUNCIATION
Good day	Buenos días	*bweh*-nohs *dee*-ahs
How are you?	¿Cómo está	*koh*-moh es-*tah*
Very well	Muy bien	mwee byehn
Thank you	Gracias	*grah*-thee-ahs
You're welcome	De nada	*deh nah*-dah
Goodbye	Adiós	ah-*dyos*
Please	Por favor	por fah-*vohr*
Yes	Sí	see
No	No	noh
Excuse me	Perdóneme	pehr-*doh*-neh-meh
Where is. . . ?	¿Dónde está. . . ?	*dohn*-deh es-*tah*
To the right	A la derecha	ah lah deh-*reh*-chah
To the left	A la izquierda	ah lah ees-*kyehr*-dah
I would like. . .	Quisiera	kee-*syeh*-rah
I want. . .	Quiero	*kyeh*-roh
Do you have. . . ?	¿Tiene usted?	tyeh-neh oo-*sted*
How much is it?	¿Cuánto cuesta?	*kwahn*-toh *kwehs*-tah
When?	¿Cuándo?	*kwahn*-doh
What?	¿Qué?	Keh
There is	(¿)Hay	aye/ee ah
(Is there. . . ?)	(. . . ?)	
What is there?	¿Qué hay?	keh aye
Yesterday	Ayer	ah-*yehr*
Today	Hoy	oy
Tomorrow	Mañana	mah-*nyah*-nah
Good	Bueno	*bweh*-noh
Bad	Malo	*mah*-loh
Better (Best)	(Lo) Mejor	(loh) meh-*hohr*
More	Más	mahs
Less	Menos	*meh*-nohs
Do you speak English?	¿Habla inglés?	ah-blah een-*glehs*

ENGLISH	SPANISH	PRONUNCIATION
I speak a little Spanish	Hablo un poco de español	*ah*-bloh oon *poh*-koh deh es-pah-*nyol*
I don't understand	No entiendo	noh ehn-*tyehn*-doh
What time is it?	¿Qué hora es?	keh *oh*-rah ehss
The check, please	La cuenta, por favor	lah *kwehn*-tah pohr fah-*vohr*
the station	la estación	lah es-tah-*syohn*
a hotel	un hotel	oon oh-*tehl*
the market	el mercado	ehl mehr-*kah*-doh
a restaurant	un restaurante	oon rehs-tow-*rahn*-teh
the toilet	el baño	ehl *bah*-nyoh
a doctor	un médico	oon *meh*-dee-koh
the road to. . .	el camino a	ehl kah-*mee*-noh ah
to eat	comer	ko-*mehr*
a room	una habitación	oo-nah ah-bee-tah-*syohn*
a book	un libro	oon *lee*-broh
a dictionary	un diccionario	oon deek-syoh-*nah*-ryoh

Numbers

NUMBER	SPANISH	PRONUNCIATION
1	uno	*oo*-noh
2	dos	dohs
3	tres	trehs
4	cuatro	*kwah*-troh
5	cinco	*theen*-koh
6	seis	says
7	siete	*syeh*-teh
8	ocho	*oh*-choh
9	nueve	*nweh*-beh
10	diez	dyehth
11	once	*ohn*-theh
12	doce	*doh*-theh
13	trece	*treh*-theh
14	catorce	kah-*tohr*-theh
15	quince	*keen*-seh
16	dieciséis	dyeh-thee-*says*
17	diecisiete	dyeh-thee-*syeh*-teh
18	dieciocho	dyeh-thee-*oh*-choh
19	diecinueve	dyeh-thee-*nweh*-beh
20	veinte	*bayn*-teh
30	treinta	*trayn*-tah
40	cuarenta	kwah-*rehn*-tah
50	cincuenta	theen-*kwehn*-tah
60	sesenta	seh-*sehn*-tah
70	setenta	seh-*tehn*-tah
80	ochenta	oh-*chehn*-tah
90	noventa	noh-*behn*-tah
100	cien	*thyehn*

Meals & Courses

ENGLISH	SPANISH	PRONUNCIATION
Breakfast	Desayuno	deh-sah-*yoo*-nooh
Lunch	Almuerzo	al-*mwehr*-thoh
Dinner	Cena	*theh*-nah
Meal	Comida	ko-*mee*-thah
Appetizers	Entremeses	en-treh-*meh*-sehs
Main course	Primer plato	pree-mehr *plah*-toh
Dessert	Postre	*pohs*-treh

Table Setting

ENGLISH	SPANISH	PRONUNCIATION
Bottle	Botella	bot-*teh*-lyah
Cup	Taza	*tah*-thah
Fork	Tenedor	teh-neh-*dor*
Glass	Vaso or Copa	*bah*-soh or *koh*-pah
Knife	Cuchillo	koo-*chee*-lyoh
Napkin	Servilleta	sehr-vi-*lye*-tah
Spoon	Cuchara	koo-*chah*-rah

Decoding the Menu

ENGLISH	SPANISH	PRONUNCIATION
Baked	Al horno	ahl *ohr*-noh
Boiled	Hervico	ehr-*vee*-thoh
Charcoal-grilled	A la brasa	ah lah *brah*-sah
Fried	Frito	*free*-toh
Grilled	A la plancha	ah lah *plan*-chah
Rare	Poco hecho	*poh*-koh eh-*choh*
Medium	Medio hecho	*meh*-dyo eh-*choh*
Well done	Muy hecho	mwee eh-*choh*
Roasted	Asado	ah-*sah*-thoh
Sauce	Salsa	*sahl*-sah
Spicy	Picante	pee-*kahn*-teh
Stew	Estofado	ess-toh-*fah*-doh

Dining Out

ENGLISH	SPANISH	PRONUNCIATION
Check/bill	Cuenta	*kwen*-tah
Waiter	Camarero (masc.)	kah-mah-*reh*-roh
	Camarera (fem.)	kah-mah-*reh*-rah

Beverages

ENGLISH	SPANISH	PRONUNCIATION
Beer	Cerveza	thehr-*veh*-thah
Coffee	Café	kah-*feh*
Milk	Leche	*leh*-cheh
Pitcher	Jarra	*hah*-rah
Tea	Té	the

ENGLISH	SPANISH	PRONUNCIATION
Water	Agua	*ah*-gwah
Wine	Vino	*bee*-noh
Red	Tinto	*teen*-toh
Rosé	Rosado	roh-*sah*-thoh
White	Blanco	blahn-*koh*
Wine list	Carta de Vinos	*kahr*-tah deh *bee*-nohs

Meat, Sausages & Cold Cuts

ENGLISH	SPANISH	PRONUNCIATION
Beef	Buey	*bway*
Duck	Pato	*pah*-toh
Meat	Carne	*kahr*-neh
Chicken	Pollo	po-lyoh
Cold meat	Fiambre	*fyam*-breh
Cutlet	Chuleta	choo-*leh*-tah
Ham	Jamón	hah-*mohn*
Cooked ham	Jamón York	hah-*mohn* york
Cured ham	Jamón Serrano	hah-*mohn* she-*rah*-noh
Lamb	Cordero	kohr-*deh*-roh
Kidneys	Riñones	ree-*nyoh*-nehs
Liver	Hígado	ee-gah-toh
Partridge	Perdiz	*pehr*-deeth
Pheasant	Faisán	fahy-*thahn*
Pork	Cerdo	*thehr*-doh
Rabbit	Conejo	koh-*neh*-hoh
Ribs	Costilla	kos-*tee*-lyah
Sausage	Salchicha	sahl-*chee*-chah
Spicy sausage	Chorizo	choh-*ree*-thoh
Steak	Bistec	*bee*-stehk
Sirloin	Solomillo	so-loh-*mee*-lyoh
Tripe	Callos	*kah*-lyohs
Turkey	Pavo	*pah*-voh
Veal	Ternera	tehr-*neh*-rah

Seafood & Shellfish

ENGLISH	SPANISH	PRONUNCIATION
Anchovy		
salt	Anchoa	ahn-*choh*-ah
fresh	Boquerón	boh-*keh*-rohn
Bass	Lubina	
Bream (porgy)	Besugo	beh-*soo*-goh
Crab	Cangrejo	kan-*greh*-hoh
Cod	Bacalao	bah-kah-*lah*-oh
Crayfish	Cigala	see-*gah*-lah
Cuttlefish	Jibia	*hih*-byah
Fish	Pescado	pess-*kah*-thoh

ENGLISH	SPANISH	PRONUNCIATION
Flounder	Platija	plah-*tee*-hah
Hake	Merluza	mehr-*loo*-thah
Grouper	Mero	*mehr*-roh
Lobster	Langosta	lahn-*goss*-tah
Mackerel	Caballa	cah-*ba*-lyah
Monkfish	Rape	*rah*-peh
Mussel	Mejillón	meh-hee-*lyohn*
Octopus	Pulpo	*pool*-poh
Oyster	Ostra	*ohs*-trah
Prawn	Gamba	*gahm*-bah
Red mullet	Salmonete	sal-moh-*neh*-teh
Salmon	Salmón	sal-*mohn*
Sardine	Sardina	sahr-*dee*-nah
Scallop	Peregrina	peh-reh-*gree*-nah
Shellfish	Mariscos	mah-*reess*-kohs
Sole	Lenguado	len-*gwah*-tho
Shrimp	Camarón	ka-mah-*rohn*
Squid	Calamar	kah-lah-*mahr*
Swordfish	Pez espada	peth ess-*pah*-thah
Trout	Trucha	*troo*-chah
Tuna	Atún	ah-*toon*
Turbot	Rodaballo	roh-dah-*ba*-lyoh

Miscellaneous

ENGLISH	SPANISH	PRONUNCIATION
Banana	Plátano	*plah*-tah-noh
Bread	Pan	pahn
Bread roll	Bollo	*bo*-lyoh
Butter	Mantequilla	mahn-the-*kee*-lyah
Caramel custard	Flan	flahn
Cheese	Queso	*keh*-soh
Egg	Huevo	*weh*-boh
Fruit	Fruta	*froo*-tah
Ice cream	Helado	eh-*lah*-doh
Omelet	Tortilla	tohr-*tee*-lya
Pepper	Pimienta	pee-*myen*-tah
Rice	Arroz	*ah*-rohth
Salt	Sal	sahl
Sugar	Azúcar	ah-*thoo*-kahr

Index

See also Accommodations and Restaurant indexes, below.

Photo **Credits**